CREATIVE HOMEOWNER®

DECK DESIGNS

PLUS ■ RAILINGS ■ PLANTERS ■ BENCHES

By Steve Cory

CREATIVE HOMEOWNER®, Upper Saddle River, New Jersey

Editorial Director: Timothy O. Bakke
Art Director: W. David Houser

Copy Editor: Douglas Cantwell
Editorial Assistants: Dan Lane, Stanley Sudol

Design and Layout: Monduane Harris, David Geer
Front Cover Design: Annie Jeon
Front Cover Photography: Kim, Jin Hong Photo Studio
Back Cover Design: W. David Houser
Back Cover Photography: John Parsekian (top),
    Jay Graham (bottom)
Illustrations: Clarke Barre (Senior Illustrator),
    Vincent Alessi, Michael Gellatly, Kathleen Rushton

Manufactured in the United States of America

Current Printing (last digit)
20 19 18 17 16 15 14 13 12 11

Deck Designs
Library of Congress Catalog Card Number: 99-62083
ISBN: 1-58011-070-3

CREATIVE HOMEOWNER®
A Division of Federal Marketing Corp.
24 Park Way, Upper Saddle River, NJ 07458
www.creativehomeowner.com

Photo Credits

Directionals: T-top, B-bottom, C-center, R-right, L-left

p. 1: David Duncan Livingston, Mill Valley, CA
p. 3T: John Parsekian, Bloomfield, NJ
p. 3 (2nd from T): Steve Budman, Norfolk, VA
p. 3 (3rd from T): Jay Graham, San Anselmo, CA
p. 3 (4th from T): California Redwood Association (Dan Sellers), Novato, CA
p. 4: California Redwood Association (Ernest Braun)
p. 6: Brian Vanden Brink, Rockport, ME
pp. 7, 8: Woody Cady, Bethesda, MD
p. 10: Samu Studios, Bayport, NY
p. 11: Tria Giovan, New York, NY
p. 12: David Duncan Livingston
p. 13: Intermatic, Inc., Spring Grove, IL
p. 14: Brian Vanden Brink
p. 16: California Redwood Association
p. 17: California Redwood Association (Ernest Braun)
p. 18: Mark Lohman, Los Angeles, CA
p. 19: Jessie Walker, Glencoe, IL
p. 20: Mark Lohman
p. 21: Jessie Walker
p. 22: California Redwood Association (Ernest Braun)
p. 23: California Redwood Association (Marvin Sloben)
pp. 24, 25, 26: Woody Cady
p. 28: Samu Studios
p. 29: Jessie Walker
p. 30: Woody Cady
p. 31: California Redwood Association (Ernest Braun)
p. 32: California Redwood Association (Marvin Sloben)
p. 34TL: Brian Vanden Brink
p. 34TR: Jessie Walker
pp. 34CR, 34BR: Woody Cady
p. 35: Samu Studios
p. 36TL: John Parsekian
p. 36BL: Jay Graham
p. 37BR: California Redwood Association (Dan Sellers)
pp. 38, 39, 40, 41, 42, 43: John Parsekian
pp. 74, 75, 76, 77, 79: Steve Budman
pp. 118, 119, 120, 121, 123: Jay Graham
pp. 158, 159: California Redwood Association (Dan Sellers)
pp. 160, 161T: Rick Parish, Plano, TX
p. 161B: California Redwood Association (Greg Hursley)
p. 163: California Redwood Association (Dan Sellers)

Table of Contents

Introduction

A deck can enhance your life in several ways. It makes entertaining easy and provides a pleasant outdoor space that you and your friends can enjoy together: just give the deck a quick sweep, prepare some cool drinks, and fire up the grill as guests gather around. For more private times, it offers a retreat where you can lounge during the day or toast the sunset, savoring the outdoors without venturing far from the amenities of civilization. A deck improves the appearance and usefulness of your home and yard by providing a smooth transition between the two. If the cost worries you, keep in mind that a high-quality deck is bound to increase your home's resale value. In the long run, this can cancel out the expense of building it—and then some.

To ensure that it enhances your property both now and in the future, a deck must be thoughtfully designed and solidly constructed of pleasing and durable materials. A poorly designed deck can cramp food preparation and dining space or create annoying traffic bottlenecks. An ill-considered choice of materials or design elements can clash with your house or yard. A poorly built deck made from inferior lumber can bounce under foot, sink over time, or rot in a few short years. Whether you intend to build the deck yourself or hire a contractor, it makes sense to spend plenty of time choosing a good design and appropriate, high-quality materials.

The first part of this book will talk you through the design process, from general ideas to specific plans. Here

◀ *A well-designed deck—made from good-quality materials using fine workmanship—will serve you well for many years and increase the value of your home.*

you'll find a selection not just of dream decks but of practical ideas that you can incorporate into any deck. The rest of the book is devoted to specific deck designs obtained

▼ *A **curved deck** with jigsaw-puzzle decking and a rounded railing, takes extra time and skill but doesn't require specialized tools or materials.*

from four designer-builders, each of whom represents a different part of the United States. These designs have been built for actual owners, all of whom have expressed enthusiastic satisfaction with them. They do not represent mere concepts or plans.

The drawings that accompany each design are based on working draw-

ings that were approved by local building inspectors. If you find that one of these decks suits all of your needs and that its dimensions fit your house and yard, you may be able simply to copy the floor plans, plot the footings and framework, and present them to your local inspector. However, because houses and yards differ and building-code require-

ments can vary, you may need to make some changes and come up with your own drawings.

Before you order materials, make sure that the design not only fits your needs but also lies within the realm of feasibility. If you're a novice and plan to build the deck yourself, you may want to avoid complicated designs. Some details, such as the laminated curved railings and benches shown on pages 40–41, require special equipment and tools. Others, such as the curved design shown on pages 106–107, will take some extra time but shouldn't pose any problems for a person skilled in the use of hand power tools.

Dream Book. Whatever your skill level, you can enjoy this book. It is intended as a deck enthusiast's dream book rather than a manual of deck projects. *None of the designs comes with a complete set of how-to instructions.* Instead, the discussion focuses on two or three interesting

and unusual aspects of each. Specific instructions for these are provided in the "Construction Techniques" sections. Often, these techniques can be applied to a variety of different designs. Sections such as "Standard Footing, Posts, and Beams" (page 116) and "Supporting a Deck Nearly Flush to the Ground" (page 84) describe procedures that you can follow regardless of the particular design you've chosen.

So, to a certain extent, you can also think of this book as a course in advanced deck-building. Don't just flip through the pages until you find the deck you want. Take a little time to examine the specific construction techniques—the extra touches as well as the fundamental approaches.

A deck can be almost anything you want it to be, but the enjoyment you'll get from it will depend largely on how much thought and energy you put into it. So read, dream, learn, . . . and most of all, enjoy!

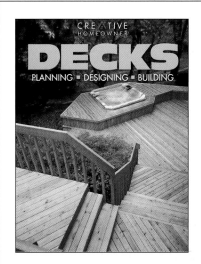

If you plan to build a deck yourself. use this book as a companion to Creative Homeowner's *Decks: Planning, Designing, Building*. In that book, you'll find detailed step-by-step instructions for all aspects of deck-building. However, if you intend to hire a contractor to build, this book can stand on it's own.

◀ *A deck serves as the transition between the privacy of your home and the outside world.*

This section will show you how to formulate the basic design of your deck: its shape, size, height, and materials. For complete instructions on how to design a durable structure that complies with code and how to make scale drawings, consult the Creative Homeowner book *Decks: Plan, Design, Build.* (See a photo of this book on page 7.)

Making Design Choices

You may feel intimidated by the design process. The language designers use often suggests an arcane discipline that can only be practiced by those with special training. While it may be true that a professional designer can offer ideas that wouldn't otherwise occur to you, anyone willing to put forth the effort can learn the basics of design. Moreover, a deck requires much less design work than a house or even an addition. You might be surprised at the ideas you and your family come up with if you spend some time examining your needs and situation.

Use Past Experience. Chances are you remember pleasant places from your past or have visions of ideal spaces for relaxing. These memories and dreams can provide images that you can shape into design concepts.

Involve the Family. Talk to your spouse and children about their future deck. Although it's best to avoid designing a deck "by committee," you'll want to consult them about their favorite activities and hear their opinions on the deck's appearance. This can actually provide an opportunity to get better acquainted with one another.

◀ *This elegant deck uses materials as part of its design statement, contrasting 2x4 redwood decking with a white railing treatment.*

▲ *An upper-level deck* serves as a second-tier front porch for this rustic home.

◀ *This grand, formal deck* provides easy access to the large, flat, usable backyard.

Work Through Drawings. Draw rough sketches as you proceed, and don't be surprised if you end up filling a wastebasket or two with them. You and your family will find it easier to talk things through if you have a drawing in front of you. You'll end up throwing away ideas that don't hold your interest, that you can't agree on, or that turn out to be impractical, but don't let false starts discourage you. In fact, expect this to happen several times before you come up with the best design.

Borrow Ideas. The best architects do not hesitate to "steal," and neither should you. Examine the decks in this book. Have a look at the decks in your neighborhood, taking photos and jotting down notes. Most neighbors will find this flattering and will gladly discuss their deck's strengths and drawbacks with you.

How Will You Use Your Deck?

Gather the family together, and discuss everyone's idea of a deck. Your kids may have friends whose families have decks—what do they like and dislike about theirs?

Take a walk around your property, and decide where the deck ought to be located. The backyard is the logical choice, but an enlarged front porch may better suit your needs.

How large a deck do you want? If a large deck would cut into your yard area, making it tough to play croquet or throwing shade on the flower bed, you may want to go minimal. But if you rarely use your yard or hate maintaining the lawn, a larger deck will make life easier.

Consider the things you typically do outdoors and how a deck could make them more enjoyable. Think about new ways to enjoy outdoor living as well. Some common activities appear on the following pages.

Barbecuing

Outdoor cooking ranks as the most popular deck activity for most people, so don't hesitate to design specifically with barbecuing in mind. Locate the grilling area as far as possible from other use areas so that you won't have to worry about kids bumping into a hot barbecue. Leave ample room for cooking "assistants" so that friends can gather around and talk as you turn the steaks. You may want to build a complete cooking center with

▲ *A separate area to the right* of the upper deck houses a built-in barbecue and provides cooking space.

▶ *A combination of low-voltage lighting* and well-placed floodlights makes this deck as useful at night as it is during the day.

counter space, cabinets, and even an outlet for a small refrigerator. If you live in an area where rain is likely to dampen your summer grilling, consider building an overhead shelter.

Dining. As you plan your deck, keep your current or future patio furniture in mind. You may want to set aside an area for a large table and chairs. If buffet eating better suits your tastes,

plan on a wide-open deck that offers several strategic, pleasant places for two or three people to gather with plates and glasses.

Seating. Built-in benches and tables may seem like a good idea, but unless you're certain that they'll comfortably accommodate all of your entertaining needs, stick with movable furniture instead. People prefer to arrange their own eating spaces, even if it means

budging their chairs only an inch or two to get situated just right.

Lighting. If you tend to eat and entertain after dark, consider your deck's lighting. A motion-sensing floodlight provides security and lights your way as you bring in groceries, but it makes for an unappealing dining ambiance. Subtle, low-voltage fixtures set into steps or posts provide a better solution. For a more festive feel, string up

some Japanese lanterns or outdoor holiday lights.

Lounging and Sunning

In choosing your deck's location, consider the following:

■ Where does the summer sun track on your yard? You'll probably want to keep the main entertaining areas away from the heat and the glare of the afternoon and setting sun.

■ Where is the best spot in the yard to sip a drink at night or to linger over the newspaper while finishing Sunday brunch?

◄ *Lounging doesn't necessarily entail sunning. Sometimes, it's just a case of enjoying the view.*

▼ *To determine how you'll use your deck, develop rough sketches to help you envision the best layout.*

■ How about the best place to work on a tan, or the perfect spot for an afternoon nap?

■ Do you want privacy, or would you prefer a place that makes it easy to keep an eye on the kids?

■ If you have a favorite hammock, lounge chair, or swinging bench, figure out the best location for it.

■ Determine the mixture of sun and shade that best suits various family members.

You'll want to take all of these factors into account when siting your deck.

Privacy

Consider whether you want a deck that feels open and expansive or one that offers seclusion and intimacy. Do you want it to provide a haven from the world or a promontory from which you can view your surroundings?

The deck's size will partially determine the approach you take, but other factors will affect its "feel" as well. Low benches and railings—or none at all—open up the deck to the yard. Railings with closely spaced balusters will give a sense of enclosure. Make the spaces wider, and the deck will tend to open outward.

Step Down or Fence in? If you build a raised deck, it might put you and your family on display for all the neighborhood to see. Rather than resign yourself to building a high fence that will give your backyard a prison-like feel, think of creative ways to achieve privacy.

Often, you can solve the problem by stepping the deck down. In most settings, decks work best when built low to the ground. If your entry door occupies a high position, you'll find it best to build a landing and stairs or a series of tiers leading down to a low-built main deck. (See "Lower Your

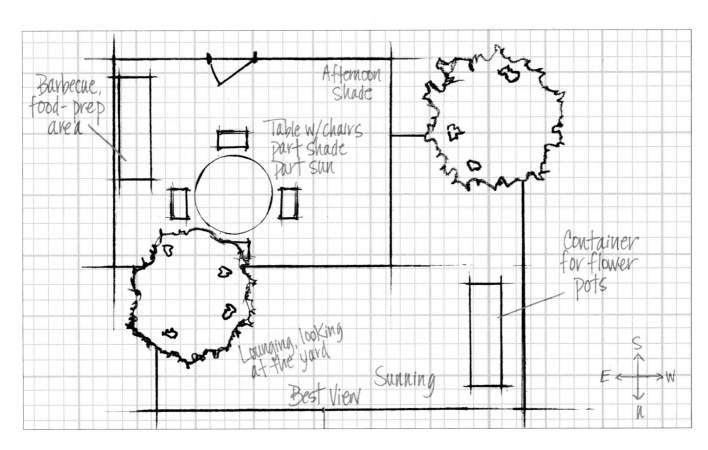

Deck for a Better View," page 27, for more information on improving views.)

As an alternative, go with a higher deck and build fence-like structures that have a friendlier appearance than a fence. A well-placed trellis can provide support for attractive climbing plants while defining an appealing enclosure. In some situations, the deck's railing may provide all the privacy you need.

Family members need some privacy among themselves as well. By building with different levels, including a conversation pit, or even by just letting the deck ramble a bit, you can make areas that are separate without being walled off.

The deck's orientation to the house will bear on its sense of privacy as well. If it hugs the house, it will have a more sequestered feel than one that juts out into the yard. For that matter,

a deck need not attach to the house at all. An island-style deck makes a clean break with the house.

In addition, consider the foliage that will surround the deck both now and later. As that nearby tree grows and spreads, your deck will feel more solitary. Hedges can provide the same enclosure as railings, whereas surrounding your deck with low-growing plants will leave it permanently exposed to the surroundings.

◀ *A handsome redwood privacy fence* and trellis create a secluded corner.

▼ *Lowering the main area* of this deck by three steps enhanced its privacy.

Planning for Children's Play

Kids spend a lot of time in the backyard, and the deck may become an important play space for them. You don't have to build a jungle gym, but you may want to design the deck to make it an inviting place for the little ones. If you add extra-wide and -deep steps, children will spend hours on them playing with dolls and trucks, letting their imaginations roam freely.

If small children will use the deck, select your materials accordingly.

Hard-edged toys can damage cedar or redwood in a hurry. Pressure-treated fir or pine will hold up better, but you'll need to sand the wood smooth to remove splinters and seal it with a penetrating finish.

A deck can also make it easier to keep an eye on the kids. If this is a concern, design the deck so that you can watch them easily from inside the house.

If the deck is more than a foot or two off the ground, you'll have to make sure any railings are childproof. Use vertical balusters spaced 4 inches on center. Even if the deck is low to the ground, you might want to install a railing if you have young children. The railing will act as a fence to keep them safe and prevent them from wandering off when you're not looking.

Enjoying Nature

Sometimes, you'll just want to sit and gaze. Orient the deck so that you can admire the best features of your yard.

If possible, plan your landscaping along with the deck to enhance this pleasure. Foliage of any kind sets off the natural tones of the wood. Think about the flowers, shrubs, climbing vines, and even trees that you might want to place near the deck. Locate bird feeders, trellises, or a small pool where they will achieve the best effect.

▼ *Thick hedges and a garden wall give this deck an intimate, room-like feeling.*

▼ *Low-growing border plants* give this deck a view
of the yard.

▲ *Wide steps* *on this yellow pine deck offer ample play space for children.*

◄ *A container garden* *of herbs, flowers, or small vegetables is ideal for a deck.*

Container Gardening. Almost anything that can be grown in your yard can also be grown in containers. With adequate sun and regular watering, practical plants such as tomatoes, peppers, and other vegetables do well in pots.

An herb garden makes an ideal deck "crop." Just a step away from the kitchen, it supplies fresh basil, parsley, and mint for your cooking, and the plants benefit from frequent clipping. Find planters that complement your deck and house, or build any of the designs shown in this book. (See, for example, planters in "Sleek Retreat," page 50; "Front Porch/ Deck for a Corner Lot," page 60; "Floating Octagons with Walkways," page 80; "Aboveground Pool Surround," page 86; "Cozy Deck with Benches and Planters," page 102.)

It's a good idea to make your container garden portable. Either build a box that will hold flower pots, or build planters that are small enough to be moved easily. That way, you can rotate flowering plants, keeping those that are currently in bloom on display to enhance the beauty of your deck.

▲ *This spa/deck combination* combines two natural materials, stone and redwood, to create an interesting design.

◀ *Small plant containers* make for easy portability.

Including a Pool or Spa

As long as you use rot-resistant, smoothly milled lumber, wood makes an excellent surround for a pool or spa. It's softer and more absorbent than tile or concrete, making it comfortable to sit on while wearing a wet swimming suit.

An inexpensive aboveground pool gains a lot of elegance when you supplement it with a deck, but compare prices before you commit yourself. You may find it only slightly more expensive to go with an in-ground pool than to install an above-grounder and build a deck.

If you decide on a whirlpool spa or hot tub, position it for privacy as well as an unobstructed view of the stars. Install comfortable seating areas around it, and remember to allow a convenient, inconspicuous place to stow the cover while using the spa.

Enhancing Your House and Yard

A deck does not stand alone. It sits near your house—usually next to it—and alters the landscape of your yard. When designing a deck, always keep its surroundings in mind. This does not necessarily mean blending the deck in with the house—it has a different structure, after all, and a different purpose. Remember, however, that contrasts ought to please the eye.

Decks literally form bridges between the indoors and outdoors. A well-designed deck should blend the two, balancing the amenities of the household with the attractions of the yard.

The Most Visible Elements

Although the lion's share of the lumber you'll install will go to the decking, this will not be the most visible element from most vantage points. People tend to see the railings, stairways, skirts, and fascia boards first. On an elevated deck, the posts and understructure may be visually prominent. In that case, a skirt will determine in large part how your deck looks to the world.

In this book, you'll find a number of railing and bench designs. (See the directory on page 186.) The companion book, *Decks: Plan, Design, Build,* presents 11 more. You can

◄ *A solid skirt* that matches the siding helps to tie this raised deck to the house.

▼ *A raised, skirted deck* can look deceptively massive.

either choose from these, create your own, or combine the features of two or more designs.

If your deck needs a skirt, choose this element carefully as well. Lattice-work makes a good choice, but a solid skirt can be made to mimic your house's siding, which helps to tie the two structures together visually.

Basic Aesthetic Considerations

To ensure that your deck harmonizes with your house and yard, you'll want to consider three factors: mass, shape, and color.

Mass. The apparent size of a deck should suit the house's dimensions. A massive-looking deck will visually overpower a small house, making it appear even smaller. A small deck that adjoins a massive exterior wall will resemble a porch.

Before you decide on the appropriate size and mass, figure out which vantage points will take precedence. How will your deck appear from the location(s) where people will most likely stand when they look at it?

A deck's visual mass does not depend solely on its size. Building it low to the ground or designing light-looking railings will cause the deck to recede and thus appear smaller. Large, visible beams, wide fascia boards, under-deck skirts, and railings made of boards rather than narrow balusters all contribute to a more massive appearance. A raised deck supported by 6x6 posts will also gain in visual mass. The higher you make the deck, the less thick the posts will appear.

You can make the house to which the deck is attached appear less massive by planting trees or tall shrubs next to it. A long exterior wall with plenty of windows and doors will appear smaller than one with large, unrelieved expanses of siding.

To increase a deck's area without making it look too big for the house, design it to hug the house rather than jut out into the yard. You might consider even wrapping the deck around a corner or two. This will make the deck appear to be a more integral part of the house rather than a stand-alone structure.

▼ *A deck that hugs the house and has a solid railing may look smaller than it really is.*

Lower Your Deck for a Better View

Many decks have a fundamental design flaw—they block the view. Railings typically stand 36 to 42 inches high, so when you look out your window, you may see them rather than the yard.

These decks may present a secondary problem if they are more than a foot or two off the ground—a highly visible under-structure, which forces you to hide it with plantings or by installing a facade of latticework. (See the drawing A at right, top.)

To improve the view, try stepping the main level of the deck down. Two steps can make a difference (drawing B at right, middle). As mentioned before, concrete footings, posts, and beams usually call for some sort of skirting, but a lower deck can eliminate this problem.

For a completely unobstructed view, lower the deck to near-ground level, preferably by stages so that it needs no railing (drawing C at right, bottom). Designing your deck in this way need not eliminate lounging or entertainment areas. As you can see in the drawing, the design provides for a landing at the doorway; a large area for barbecuing, dining, and lounging; and a transitional area to the yard—essentially a wide bottom step. The design also eliminates any view of the understructure.

As an alternative, install see-through railings to improve the view. (See "Railing with Shingles and Glassed Section," page 144.)

▲ *This luxurious backyard deck* complements the curves of the house's turret-like structure.

▶ *The lines of this deck,* which extends out into a private yard, help it blend into the landscape.

Shape. The shape you choose should not mimic your house, but it should complement it. A simple, straightforward deck can soften a complex house design, whereas a boldly curved or angled deck can enliven a plain-looking house. On the other hand, if your house has an interesting but simple shape—an "L" for example—you may want to repeat that.

In general, a deck looks best if it has a horizontal rather than vertical configuration. Strong horizontal lines tend to emphasize the impression of an informal space. If you must raise the deck, try to soften the inevitably vertical lines, perhaps by making the skirt out of horizontal boards.

Most people choose to locate a deck at the rear of the house, but consider other options. A deck can wrap around two, three, or even four walls, offering a choice of different views as well as more possibilities for seclusion. A deck can form a peninsula, extending out via a walkway to become more a part of the yard than of the house. You can even build an island that doesn't attach to the house at all.

Give some thought to individual lines and design details as well. If your house has distinctive curves, projec-

tions, or angles, you may want to reiterate them on your deck. If your house has uninteresting lines, use the deck to add variety, such as octagons, diagonals, or curves. Take care, however, that you don't go overboard. Two or three such details artfully

arranged and perhaps repeated make for a pleasing design.

Color. Most homeowners think of a deck as an informal space that ought to project a mood of warmth and relaxation. To enhance this, it's best to stain the entire structure a natural redwood or cedartone color, or let it "go gray" and turn a rustic, silvery hue. Whichever way you go, remember to coat the deck with a preservative sealer (clear or pigmented) every year or two.

If you prefer a more formal look, consider painting part of the deck (just the railing, for instance). A white railing against dark decking looks elegant. For more contrast with the house, use a darker stain, especially if the house has light-colored siding.

◀ *This deck has discrete areas for cooking, dining, relaxing, and enjoying the spa, but also allows room for convenient traffic flow.*

▼ *A series of wide steps and landings makes this redwood deck seem part of the yard.*

Painting the entire deck is usually not a good idea, because paint can chip and peel and will wear quickly in high-traffic areas.

Accommodating Activities

Plan your deck with practicality in mind: Where will you eat? Where will you prepare and cook food? Is there a good place for informal conversation? How about for lounging? And very important: is there room for traffic to flow without interrupting these everyday pursuits?

A good deck design does not have obvious "zones" marked out for each activity, but it does provide ample room for all of them. It also takes into account the location of entry door(s). Sometimes, repositioning the deck just a few feet this way or that suddenly frees up space for a table and chairs or a walkway.

Incorporating the Yard

As a man-made structure, a deck intrinsically contains elements of the indoors. To make a graceful transition to the yard, it often helps to bring some of the outdoors onto the deck.

Creating Landings. When possible, use a series of landings to reach the lawn rather than a straightforward stairway. It often looks best to make the levels cascade—that is, fall away from the preceding level at different points and angles—rather than descend uniformly. If you'd rather stick with a standard stairway approach, modify it by making the steps both wider and deeper. Any of these techniques will make the deck more a part of the yard than strictly a means of getting to it.

Make Use of Plants and Trees. Consider building planters into your deck, or at least plan on plenty of potted plants. Flowers rarely clash with anything, nor do green or silvery leaves. As long as you keep them healthy, plants will almost certainly make your deck a more inviting place. If you make planters from the same material as that used for the deck, so much the better.

If there's a tree standing right where you want to put the deck, consider building around it rather than cutting it down. Just remember to allow ample room for growth. If you're planning a low deck, think about incorporating a large boulder into the design or leaving a small space open for shrubs or tall flowers. This adds a focal point and enhances the transition between house and landscape.

▶ *By incorporating a tree, this handsome redwood deck makes the sloped yard usable.*

A deck does not have to lead directly to a lawn. Consider making a pathway out of natural brick, stone, or concrete pavers. Even crushed stone can work well if it is thoroughly compacted and you don't expect heavy traffic or small children to use the path.

Theme & Variation

After you've looked through this book, you may have dozens of ideas that you'd like to incorporate into your new deck. However, this is the time to exercise restraint, or you'll likely end up with a confused or busy design. To achieve a sense of unity, limit yourself to one or two major themes, and then work out variations on them.

Themes

A *theme* can be a curved line, an octagonal or diagonal shape, or an unusual decking pattern. Don't use it just once—repeat it in several areas, varying the size and orientation, in order to tie the whole structure together.

If you plan to combine benches and railing with any kind of overhead structure, use common design elements in them. Guests may not consciously appreciate that the trellis partially mimics the railing, but they'll have a general sense that the two elements harmonize. If you're building a table or counter, you can make it part of the ensemble by using the same lumber that will go into the decking and assembling it in a similar pattern.

Keep in mind that the most visible parts of a deck are those with vertical lines—the benches and railings, planters, fascia, and overheads. These, more than the decking elements, need to complement each other.

Focal Points

The final step in designing not just a good but a great deck is to come up with a stunning point of interest, something that immediately catches your guests' attention. You may already have one and not recognize it: a beautiful tree, a charming view, a statue, a display of potted flowers. You might think about purchasing a more functional focal piece—a brick barbecue or an inviting hot tub. As a more artistic alternative, consider laying the decking in a distinctive pattern that converges at a point, or adding carved or sculpted railings.

Whatever your focal point, play up to it. Position the deck and your furniture so that guests' eyes will be drawn to it. Arrange lighting to make it visible at night as well.

Details

The details in a deck—workmanship, use of materials, sizing of dimensional lumber—can enhance the theme of a deck and strengthen the design. A deck that takes into account relative sizes of deck features, such as balusters and bench members, exhibits careful design. And a deck with exceptional workmanship, in the form of plugged screw holes, close-fitting joinery, and rounded, softened edges, gives the impression of good design almost irregardless of its other elements. Combined with good overall design sense, such a deck is flawless.

As you plan, don't think in terms of a deck that will merely do the job. Work to find a design that goes three steps further: it should provide a comfortable center for family gatherings and relaxation, a functional yet eye-pleasing space for entertaining friends, and a retreat for restful contemplation. In other words, create a deck that will make all facets of your life less stressful and more enjoyable.

▲ *The focal point* for this deck is the spectacular view of the Maine coastline (above left).

▶ *Sometimes successful design is in the details* (clockwise from right): the back of the bench on this Virginia seaside deck is built from the same-dimension lumber as the rail balusters; a floating handrail and contrasting paint present a handsome geometric quality; fine wood and workmanship has a furniture quality about it; soft edges and tight miters create a neat appearance.

Bob Kiefer

Gary Marsh

George Drummond

Rick Parish

Creative Homeowner selected four of the country's premier deck designer-builders and asked them to present some of their best designs to our readers. They represent a broad regional sampling: George Drummond lives in Virginia; Bob Kiefer in New Jersey; Gary Marsh in California; and Rick Parish in Texas. Their decks, many of them design award-winners, appear on the following pages.

These professionals don't just design decks—they build them as well. They recognize that a superior design addresses questions of engineering and craftsmanship as well as aesthetics. They know that a structurally sound deck requires good footings and strong framing, that a handsome, durable structure calls for careful joinery and attention to detail.

For each of the designer-builders, you'll find a description of his general approach. Then, a section called "Techniques to Use" summarizes specific tips and tricks that each has learned through years of practice and experience. Even if you choose not to build one of their decks, you'll find ideas here that you can apply to your own choice of design and construction strategy.

We hope you enjoy leafing through this impressive collection of designs and ideas. We also wish you luck in achieving your dream deck. The designer-builders welcome consultation by telephone should you be interested in their work or should you want to purchase plans for one of their designs.

◄ *Samples of the builders' work show their high degree of craftsmanship.*

DECKS *by* KIEFER

Bob Kiefer
Decks by Kiefer
Pittstown, New Jersey
908/735-8051

Bob Kiefer, owner of Decks by Kiefer in Hunterton County, New Jersey, has worked in the building trades for over 20 years. He has concentrated on decks for 11 of those years. Kiefer's clientele tends to be demanding and upscale; he rarely builds a deck for less than $10,000.

Design Considerations

Kiefer has studied landscape architecture in college, so he enjoys designing as well as building decks. Rather than relying on computer programs, he simply sits down with clients in their home and works up general sketches of the deck's basic lines. He also asks them to look through his extensive portfolio, where they sometimes find a design that they want to duplicate for themselves. "However," says Kiefer, "I don't hesitate to tell them if I think they're wrong." He's found that impromptu decisions often result in mistakes.

Kiefer begins by asking about the customers' needs: dining space, room to lounge, conversation areas, entertainment requirements, and so on. He asks not only how many guests they typically entertain at a party but also how they are likely to use their deck

◀ *Before embarking on a design,* *Bob Kiefer interviews his clients to* *understand their special require-* *ments. Some customers might want* *a cooking/barbecue area (left);* *others may have problem-solving* *needs, such as easy access to a* *remote pond (right); while others* *might just want a place for a relax-* *ing whirlpool or hot tub (below).*

on a typical day when it's "just family." To get a better feel for their personal tastes, he takes a look at the furnishings they've chosen for their home.

Once Kiefer has determined the number and approximate dimensions of the various use areas, he uses simple squares and circles to rough out the deck's shape. The style of the house often dictates these lines—an angular, contemporary house, for example, usually calls for an angular rather than a curved design. But to a large extent, Kiefer relies on intuition: "Often, the right shape just hits me as I look at the house."

Lumber Considerations

For the visible portions of most decks, Kiefer uses expensive B-grade heart redwood. "B-grade" indicates that the lumber contains tiny knots on one side only. He steers clear of "common"-graded lumber, which contains cream-colored sapwood. Not only does it detract from the deck's appearance, but it lacks the rot resistance of heartwood.

Dry Wood. For most of the deck, Kiefer finds that air-dried lumber with a moisture content of 17 percent or less provides adequate stability. For more sensitive parts, such as curved rails, he uses kiln-dried clear heartwood with a moisture content of 3 percent or less. This lumber will not shrink or twist appreciably and is much less likely to crack or splinter. Material of this quality needs little nailing. Look closely at his redwood decks, and you'll see only one fastener per joist set in an alternating pattern, except at joints, where he uses two.

Exotic Wood. On some decks, Kiefer uses ipé, a South American ironwood that costs even more than redwood. (An environmental note: Although ipé grows in the rain forest, it is a rapid-growing tree that is not endangered, so using it probably does less ecological damage than using redwood. Companies that supply ipé claim that if harvested responsibly, it is easily replenishable.) This material offers remarkable durability and rot-resistance, although its hardness makes it difficult to work. Every screw requires a pilot hole. However, Kiefer goes even further, drilling and counterboring pilot holes and then driving stainless-steel screws. He then fills each hole with a plug cut from scrap wood. (See photo at right.) This painstaking process yields a rugged but clean-looking deck surface.

For curved benches and railings, Kiefer sometimes uses a laminating

process that exceeds the means of most do-it-yourselfers. (See "Bench with Laminated Curved Seat Members," page 53.) The work itself is not that demanding, but the technique requires up to 100 clamps and a large workspace. If you plan to build the deck yourself, you may be able to find a mill shop that will do the curved-bench work for you.

Kiefer suggests waiting a month before applying a finish to redwood to allow the tannins to leach out. If a client neglects to finish a deck, and the redwood turns gray, all is not lost. He simply cleans the wood with a deck cleaner and applies the stain or other finish. Ipé contains so much natural oil that it will not accept stains, but it can be treated with a clear sealer. Clean the wood every year or at least every two years, and apply a new coat of sealer.

▲ **Kiefer uses 2x4 decking**—*typical of most of his decks—on this beautiful redwood version.*

◀ **Look closely at the decking** *and at the railing, and you'll see a common Kiefer trademark: plugged fastener holes.*

Techniques to Use

For his well-to-do clients, Kiefer usually spares no expense to ensure that a deck will withstand warping and cracking for decades. Although economy may factor into your project, you can still use Kiefer's ideas and techniques to add strength and elegance to your deck.

▶ Kiefer prefers 2x4 redwood (or 1x4 ipé) for decking, whereas most builders use (nominal) 6-inch-wide stock. The narrow boards account in part for the distinctive appearance of his decks. However, if you use a grade of lumber that contains knots, 2x4s can present a problem. If you end up with a large knot in a location that requires a nail, you won't have room to work around it as you would with 2x6 decking. By using lumber that has virtually no knots, you can eliminate this problem.

▶ Wherever possible, Kiefer avoids miter cuts in decking and rail caps. He's found that any slight imperfection or shrinkage will mar the appearance of a mitered joint. Instead he uses square cuts, staggering them in the decking to create a pleasing herringbone pattern.

▶ Kiefer steers clear of end-to-end butt joints along the length of the decking. These joints often crack because the boards must be nailed so close to their ends. If shrinkage occurs, unsightly gaps can result. Where feasible, he uses 20-foot-long decking runs (or 18-foot if 20-footers are not available). To avoid overly long decking on larger areas, he usually chooses to install boards in a herringbone pattern.

▶ To install structural posts, Kiefer uses an unconventional approach. (See page 48.) By waiting until the deck is nearly completed before pouring concrete, he avoids errors in footings that can make building the rest of the deck a nightmare.

▶ For structural support, he uses lumber no larger than 2x10. Larger pieces tend to shrink and crack. Kiefer's beam design is simplicity itself: he gang-nails three 2x10s to form a support that is considerably stronger and much less likely to crack than a 4x10.

▶ He usually builds rail posts out of 2x4s and 1x4s. They assemble easily, resist cracking, and look more elegant than a 4x4. (See photo oppposite and page 49.)

▶ To achieve the distinctive banded appearance of his fascias, Kiefer stacks several 2x4s rather than using a single 1x8 as most builders would. The 2x4s don't crack as readily as the wider, thinner boards, and the round milled edges on the 2x4s accent the horizontal lines between the boards. To economize, you can use 1x4s and round the edges with a sanding block or a router equipped with a roundover bit.

▶ Kiefer makes curved fascia under the decking using a technique that is feasible for anyone who owns a decent table saw. (See page 58.) However, his laminated curved benches and railings may prove too difficult for the average do-it-yourselfer. (See page 53.)

◀ *By fastening 2x4s and 1x4s together, Kiefer crafts handsome, unusual-looking posts.*

▶ *To avoid butt joints and miter cuts, Kiefer often uses shorter decking boards and herringbone patterns. Also note the distinctive banded design of the fascia, repeated on many of his decks.*

Tilted Square

ere, Kiefer uses a basic shape to create a deck that feels not the least bit squarish yet still satisfies the eye with its clean, uncluttered lines.

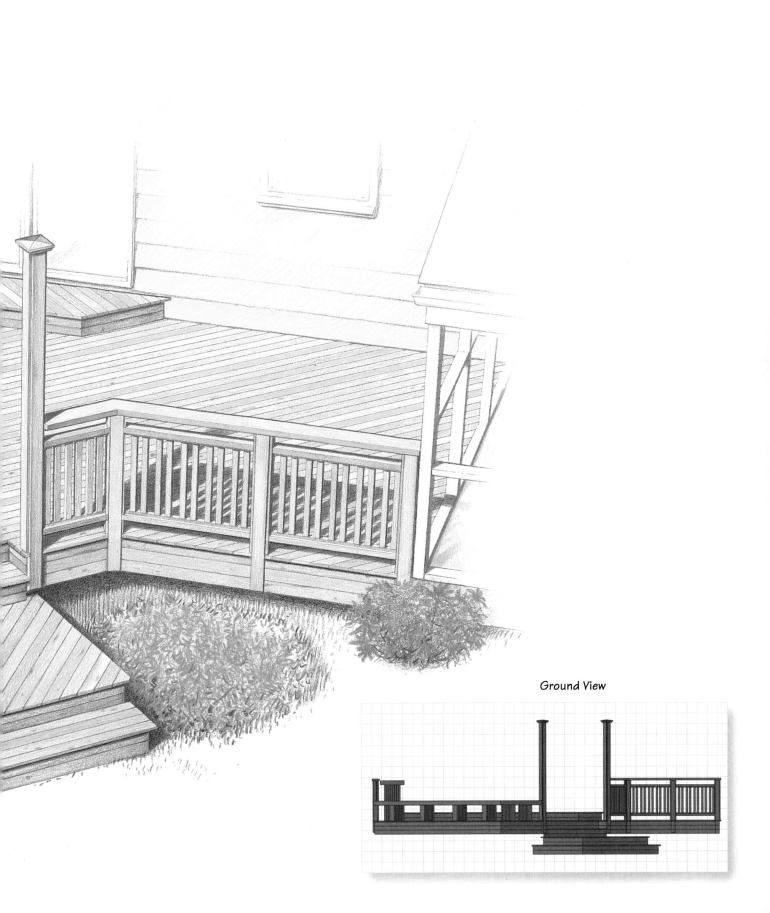

Ground View

Tilted Square, Plan View

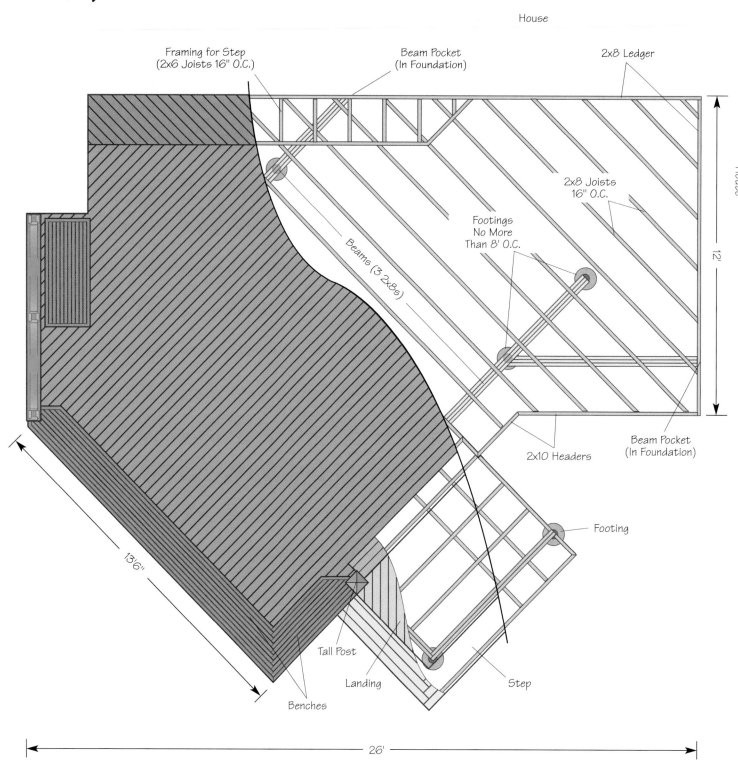

House

Framing for Step
(2x6 Joists 16" O.C.)

Beam Pocket
(In Foundation)

2x8 Ledger

House

2x8 Joists
16" O.C.

Footings
No More
Than 8' O.C.

Beams (3 2x8s)

12'

13'6"

2x10 Headers

Beam Pocket
(In Foundation)

Footing

Tall Post

Landing

Step

Benches

26'

Design Considerations

The goal of this project was to turn a 14-foot square surface diagonally in relation to the house. Once the empty spaces were filled in, the deck's shape emerged. A plan like this works well in a wide yard where the view does not need to be directed straight back from the house. It encourages people to look out across the yard in two directions, and at the same time gives the deck a more enclosed feel than it would have as a standard rectangle perpendicular to the house.

Kiefer talks about "getting the deck into the yard," by which he means extending the deck enough to bring it down gradually to grade level. This enhances the sense that the deck forms a bridge from the house to the yard. By stepping down two levels to a

landing rather than offering a simple stairway to the yard, this deck makes a smooth transition.

Outside the sliding kitchen doors, Kiefer built a stepped-down area that has benches instead of railings. This makes it easy to gaze from the kitchen into the yard and provides guests with an unobstructed view even from low lounge furniture.

The areas to each side of the doors, designed for barbecuing and dining, do have railings. Even though this deck is not elevated enough to require it, a railing gives the eating area a sense of enclosure. Guests seated at a table can see over it with little difficulty, and the rail provides support for a food-preparation table.

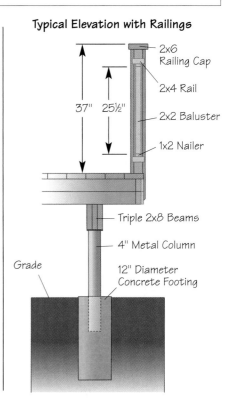

Typical Elevation with Railings

2x6 Railing Cap
2x4 Rail
2x2 Baluster
1x2 Nailer
37" 25½"
Triple 2x8 Beams
4" Metal Column
Grade
12" Diameter Concrete Footing

Materials Used for This Deck

Framing	Tripled 2x8s for beams 2x8 ledgers and joists 2x10 header joists 2x6 joists for bottom landing		Spacers made from scrap two-by lumber Small bundle of cedar shims
Decking	2x4s	Hardware	Concrete-filled metal columns, painted, with screws for attaching to beams Lag screws and washers for installing ledger board pieces Joist hangers for 2x8s Angled joist hangers for 2x8s Angle brackets 1/2" x 4" lag screws with washers for rail posts Fasteners for joist hangers 2½" deck screws or 10d galvanized nails Framing straps
Fascia	2x4s		
Railing	2x4 post pieces 1x4 post pieces 2x6 railing cap 2x4 top and bottom rails 2x2 balusters 1x2 nailers 2x8 for tops of tall posts		
Bench	2x2 seat pieces 2x4 edging 2x6 legs	Masonry	Concrete Concrete tube forms

Construction Techniques

This deck displays many of Kiefer's characteristic design features: banded fascia, beams set in pockets in the house, concrete-filled metal posts (Lally columns), rails made from paired 2x2 balusters, posts made from 1x4s and 2x4s, the bench design, and the herringbone decking pattern. But because it has no curves, the deck poses fewer challenges to the do-it-yourselfer than most of Kiefer's other creations.

Cutting Beam Pockets

The beams are anchored in pockets cut into the house's foundation walls. In most cases, this will require cutting holes in concrete or other masonry. To do this job quickly, rent or buy a diamond blade for your circular saw. To save money (but not time), you can drill multiple holes with a masonry bit and then chip out the hole with a cold chisel.

First, mark for the ledger and determine the beam pocket locations. The tops of the beams should butt up against the bottoms of the ledgers. Next, cut the pockets in the foundation wall(s). Because one of the beams enters the house at an angle, you'll have to widen that hole by about $^3/_4$ inch. Slightly oversize the holes vertically as well (by about $^1/_8$ inch) so that you won't have to struggle to insert the beams.

Install the ledger pieces and flashing. With a step at the entry door like this, the ledger should measure at least $7^3/_4$ inches below the threshold to allow room for a 2x6 joist ($5^1/_2$ inches

high), 2x4 decking ($1^1/_2$ inches thick), and at least $^3/_4$ inch to keep melting snow out.

Construct the Beams. Lay one 2x8 on top of another, checking to make sure that they crown in the same direction. Join the two boards using $2^1/_2$-inch screws or 10d spiral-shank galvanized nails, placed every 6 inches in an alternating pattern. Attach a third board in the same way, but *use longer fasteners.* Do not cut the beams to exact size—you'll do that later. However, go ahead and trim the ends that will enter the house diagonally to a 45-degree angle, stacking the boards to yield a total end cut of 45 degrees. This will make it easier to poke the beam into the pocket.

Hanging the Columns

Dig 12-inch-diameter holes for the footings to a depth that exceeds the frost line (or to at least 24 inches). If desired, install concrete tube forms as well. Start with the long beam that enters the house at an angle. Recruit a

Hanging Columns

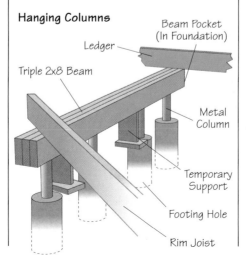

Beam Pocket (In Foundation)
Ledger
Triple 2x8 Beam
Metal Column
Temporary Support
Footing Hole
Rim Joist

helper or two, and insert one end into the beam pocket; then check to make sure its top edge butts up against the bottom of the ledger. (You may need to add shims.) Set a level on top of the beam to determine the length of your temporary supports; then cut and install them as shown.

If the beam feels wobbly, angle a 2x4 brace down from it to the ground, and attach the brace to a stake. Install the second long beam level with the first, and temporarily support it the same way. Cut the small beam to fit, and then slide it into the pocket. Attach the small beam to the other beam using angle brackets. Once the beams are in place, immediately install two or three joists to keep the structure stable.

Attach the concrete-filled metal columns to the undersides of the beams; then check to make sure that they hang down at least 8 inches into the footing holes. You can pour the footing concrete now or wait until you've finished the framing.

Step and Landing Construction

Rather than digging and pouring footings for the rear portion of the lower landing, Kiefer connects the joists to the upper-deck framing. (See the framing detail opposite.) Although this method produces a sound structure, some building departments may not approve it, so check with your local inspector. The outer corners of the landing are supported by normal concrete footings.

Step and Landing Framing Detail

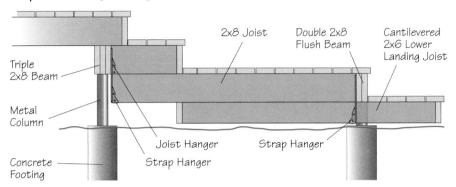

Triple 2x8 Beam

Metal Column

Concrete Footing

Strap Hanger

Joist Hanger

2x8 Joist

Double 2x8 Flush Beam

Strap Hanger

Cantilevered 2x6 Lower Landing Joist

Construct the Step and Landing Area. At the front end of the bottom step, pour concrete footings to support the double 2x8 flush beam. At the rear end, use long framing strap hangers to tie the step and landing framing to the main framing as shown. You may of course need to construct more or fewer steps, depending on the height of your deck.

Building the Rail Posts and Balustrade

Construct the rail posts from 2x4s and 1x4s as shown at right. Attach the pieces to form a consistent $^3/_4$-inch reveal at each corner.

Determine the post locations carefully to ensure uniform spacing between them. Cut notches in the decking just large enough to allow

snug (not tight) insertion of the posts. Check the posts for plumb; then attach them using 4-inch lag screws.

Cut the top and bottom 2x4 rails and 1x2 nailers to fit between the posts. Cut the 2x2 balusters to $25^1/_2$ inches long, and then construct the balustrade sections as shown below. Build each of these as a unit on a flat surface as if you were constructing a ladder. Because you'll use an alternating spacing for the balusters, as shown in the drawing, you must lay out the entire section first to ensure that you don't end up with odd-sized spaces at the ends. You may choose to vary the gaps between the balusters to suit your tastes and to make them come out even on the sides. Now slide the balustrade sections in, and attach them to the posts with angle-driven screws. Finish the rail by installing the 2x6 railing caps.

Cover the tops of the tall posts with post caps. (See the rendering for the tall post locations.) You can purchase decorative caps like that shown from a well-stocked lumberyard or millwork center, although skilled woodworkers could make them from 2x8 stock on a table saw. (See page 67 for the basic procedure.) Rip a length of scrap stock to $^3/_4$ x $^3/_4$ inches, and cut it into four lengths to fit on top of the post under the cap as shown. Then center and nail a cap to the top of each post.

Railing Posts

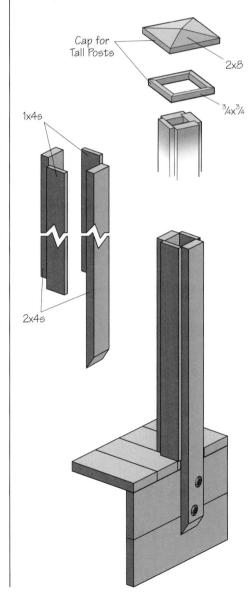

Cap for Tall Posts

2x8

$^3/_4$x$^3/_4$

1x4s

2x4s

Balustrade Section

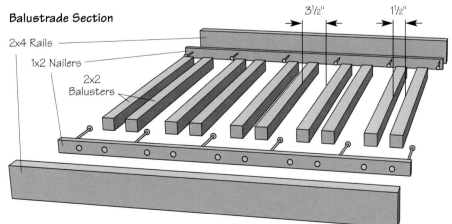

2x4 Rails

1x2 Nailers

2x2 Balusters

$3^1/_2$" $1^1/_2$"

Sleek Retreat

ith its sinuous curves, this handsome deck may remind you of an appliance or car from the 1950s. The natural softness of the wood makes it a relaxing place to withdraw from the world, however briefly.

Ground View

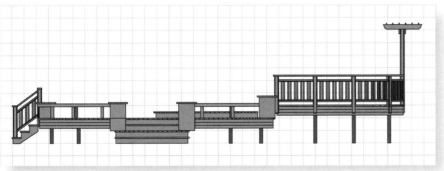

Design Considerations

The deck's smooth lines emphasize the curved, banded fascia. The overall effect contrasts markedly with most (rectangular) houses in style and materials, yet the horizontal lines harmonize well with the siding found commonly on today's homes.

From the house, you step onto an upper level designed as a barbecue area that will accommodate a table and chairs. This 13x20-foot space provides generously for traffic flow. An overhead trellis offers support for hanging flower baskets or climbing vines and provides shade for a table and chairs that you might set up for dining.

A wide, curved step leads to the lower level, which projects farther into the yard. Here there is no railing to obstruct the view, and the ample space allows for plenty of general seating and entertaining. Three large planters bring foliage onto the deck. Curved benches tie into the planters and follow the deck's contours. This stunning element presents a challenging project to the amateur carpenter, so it may be worth the expense to hire a professional.

Instead of simply stepping the deck down to the yard, Kiefer includes a small landing as part of the stairway. This extends the deck farther outward, making a smoother transition from deck to yard. The elevated landing makes a pleasant place to sit and sip a drink. A second, standard-size stairway next to the house allows more convenient daily traffic flow to and from the yard.

Sleek Retreat, Plan View

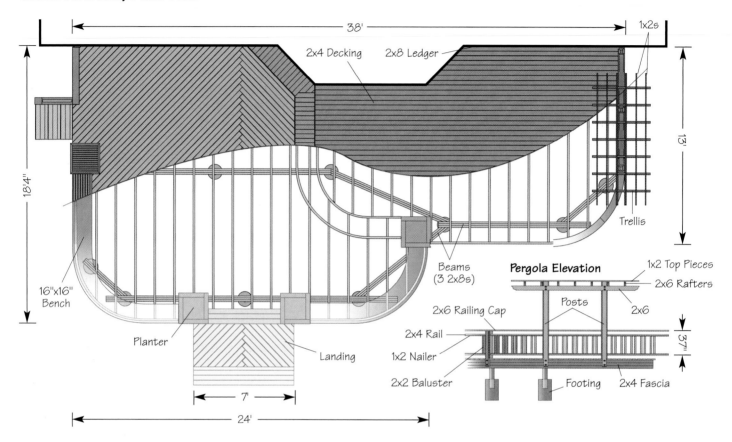

Materials Used for This Deck

Framing	Tripled 2x8s for beams 2x8 joists 2x8 ledger pieces and headers	Benches	2x4s for supports 2x4 seat pieces, ripped to $5/16$" and laminated
Decking	2x4s	Planters	2x6 framing pieces 2x6 floor pieces 1x6 tongue-and-groove sides 2x4 top trim
Fascia	2x4s; curved pieces ripped to $5/16$" and laminated		
Railing	2x4 post pieces 1x4 post pieces 2x12s for curved top and bottom rails Doubled 1x12s for curved railing cap 1x6s for curved nailers 2x4 straight top and bottom rails 1x2 nailers 2x6s for straight railing cap 2x2 balusters 2x2 handrails	Hardware	Concrete-filled metal posts Lag screws and washers for installing ledgers Joist hangers for 2x10s Angle brackets Fasteners for joist hangers 3" deck screws or 10d galvanized nails $1/2$" x $3 1/2$" lag screws with washers, for posts
Overhead structure (Pergola)	(posts shared with railing) 2x6 double beams 2x6 rafters 1x2 top pieces	Masonry	Concrete Concrete tube forms

Construction Techniques

Install pocket beams and Lally columns as described on page 48. To frame the curved section, see page 58. Other techniques used are more specific to this deck.

Building a Curved Railing

The straight sections of railing are built ladder-style as described on page 49.

Mark for the post locations on the curve, but do not install them. To make the top and bottom rails, lay pieces of 2x12 on the deck, and use the round decking edge to mark them for curved rip cuts, keeping the width of the pieces at a uniform $3^1/2$ inches. Cut each section a little longer than needed. Use these pieces to mark for the curved nailers, which you'll cut to a consistent $1^1/2$-inch width. Use the same technique to make curved one-by pieces for the top rail. These

Pergola

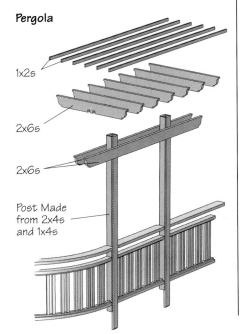

1x2s

2x6s

2x6s

Post Made from 2x4s and 1x4s

should measure $5^1/2$ inches wide and as long as you can make them.

Install the posts, and then cut the rails and nailers to fit between them. Install the rails, assemble the nailers and balusters, and then attach the baluster subassemblies to the rails. The nailers make it easier to position the balusters centered on the top and bottom rails and add a bit of strength. **Note:** You can't build these sections ladder-style on the ground, because they won't lie flat.

For the railing cap, cut the bottom one-by pieces so that they center on the posts, and attach them with screws. Cut the top pieces so that the joints fall at least 12 inches from those in the bottom pieces. To attach them, apply exterior woodworking glue and drive $1^1/4$-inch screws up through the bottom pieces.

Handrail

In many areas of the country, handrails are required on stairways of three or more steps. Handrails should measure between $1^1/4$ and 2 inches in diameter. In this case Kiefer used 2x2s, which fill the bill nicely. Make sure that there is enough clearance to really grasp the handrail, and then anchor it securely by driving

Handrail

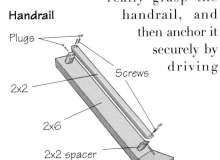

Plugs

2x2

Screws

2x6

2x2 spacer

screws through the 2x6. The design is straightforward. Choose clear lumber, and sand it smooth. Drill pilot holes for all screws to prevent the small pieces from splitting.

Bench with Laminated Curved Seat Members

Make no mistake, as handsome as it is, this bench is difficult to build. You'll have to resaw a number of pieces from 2x4s, preferably using a table saw, to produce strips that measure $5/16$ to $3/8$ inch thick and $3^1/2$ inches wide. Then you'll laminate five or six of these strips to form each bench slat. (Laminate the curved portions of the fascia in the same way.) **Note:** Cut the 2x4s longer than you'll need so that the assembled bench slats won't end up short.

To make a gluing form, cut pieces of plywood that match the curve of the deck. Then laminate the strips together using epoxy, clamping them to the curved form every 6 inches. You'll need to use lots of clamps—in all likelihood more than 100. Take care that you cover every strip thoroughly with epoxy, or the slats may delaminate. Allow the assembly to dry for 24 hours; then belt-sand the edge.

Each bench seat consists of eight slats spaced about $3/8$ inch apart. Nine $12^1/2$-inch-long laminated 2x4s form the seven vertical supports, four on one bench and three on the other. These are spaced equidistant from one another and approximately 12 inches from (and perpendicular to) the planters/tables on each end.

Raised Deck
with Sweeping Overlook

*T*he backyard of this house slopes steeply down to a lovely pond. The homeowners needed a stairway down to the pool in the side yard and wanted a clear view of the pond. To accommodate them, Kiefer built a set of stairs off to the side and a round balcony that overlooks the pond.

Ground View

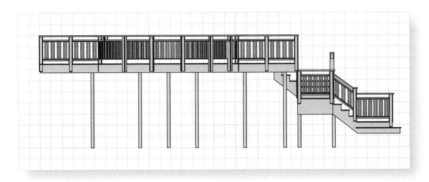

Design Considerations

When the homeowners met with Kiefer, they requested a generously sized deck but not a particularly expansive one. For large parties, they intended to entertain below by the pool. The deck design had to provide room for a standard patio table with four chairs as well as a barbecue area, without impeding the traffic down to the poolside. The central, offset semicircular area measures about 8 feet in diameter—room enough for the out-of-the-way dining area. It also makes a nice vantage point from which to lean on the rail and admire the pond below.

At 12 steps down, a simple, straight stairway would have jutted far out into the yard. Even a stairway with one landing would have protruded too far to suit the homeowners' tastes. Building *two* upper landings took extra work but proved well worth the effort, keeping the steps close to the deck. The third landing at the bottom provides a small conversation area or a space for potted plants.

One small vertical area just above the middle landing is covered with skirting, while the rest of the deck's underside is left exposed. Although it may seem desirable to have concealed some of the framing, a skirt that large would have made the deck appear box-like and would have added considerably to the expense.

A curved balcony like this one creates a dramatic effect, especially when elevated high in the air. The combination of circles and rectangles looks almost Victorian.

The high elevation makes the framing go slowly and involves some danger as well. If you are not accustomed to this type of construction, consider hiring a contractor to at least build the framing. Holding the beams temporarily in place while you install the rest of the framing is difficult work.

Raised Deck with Sweeping Overlook, Plan View

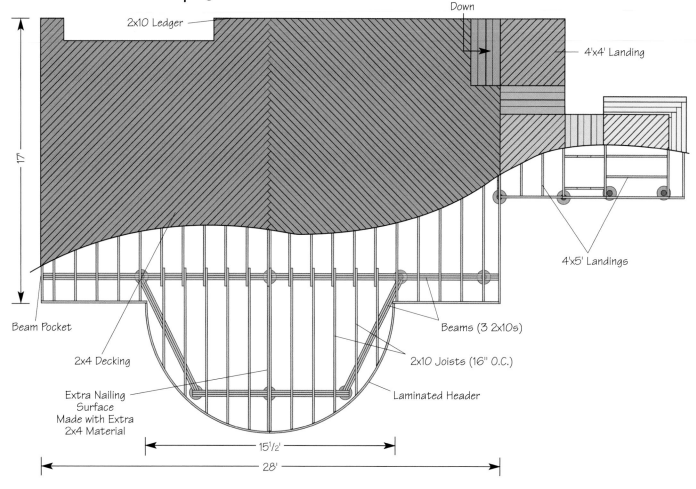

Down

2x10 Ledger

4'x4' Landing

17'

4'x5' Landings

Beam Pocket

Beams (3 2x10s)

2x4 Decking

2x10 Joists (16" O.C.)

Extra Nailing
Surface
Made with Extra
2x4 Material

Laminated Header

15½'

28'

<table>
<tr><td colspan="2" align="center">**Materials Used for This Deck**</td></tr>
<tr><td>Framing</td><td>Tripled 2x10s for beams
2x10 joists
2x10 ledger pieces and headers
2x4 redwood for curved header/fascia
2x6 stairway joists
2x12 stringers</td></tr>
<tr><td>Decking</td><td>2x4s</td></tr>
<tr><td>Fascia,
skirting,
step risers</td><td>1x6 skirting
1x4 fascia pieces
1x4 riser pieces</td></tr>
<tr><td>Railing</td><td>2x4 post pieces
1x4 post pieces
2x12s for curved top and bottom rails
Doubled 1x12s for curved railing cap
1x6s for curved nailers
2x4 straight top and bottom rails
1x2 nailers</td></tr>
</table>

	2x6 railing cap 2x2 balusters 2x2 handrails
Hardware	Concrete-filled metal columns, primed, with screws for attaching to beams Lag screws and washers for installing ledgers Joist hangers for 2x10s Angle brackets Fasteners for joist hangers 3" deck screws or 10d spiral-shank galvanized nails $1/2$" x $3^1/2$" lag screws with washers for posts
Masonry	Concrete Concrete tube forms

Construction Techniques

Installing Beams High In the Air

Anchor the ledger pieces for the main deck to the house $2^1/4$ inches or so below the level of the interior floor at the threshold. Mark for the end joist that butts the house, and determine the beam pocket's location. Using a circular or reciprocating saw (or both), cut the pocket $4^5/8$ inches wide and $9^1/4$ inches long. Then install the end joist, but don't install the ledgers for the top landing yet.

Now comes the tricky part. (Have at least two strong-backed helpers on hand, and use stable stepladders or sturdy scaffolding.) Build the long beam from three 2x10s, using stock that measures a foot or so longer than it needs to be. On a 16-foot 2x10, make a mark showing the distance the beam should be from the house; you will use this piece as a temporary brace. (See the drawing "Bracing and Supporting the Beams.") Insert the beam into the beam pocket; then raise the other end to make it level. Install plenty of bracing, using more than shown if necessary.

Once you've securely anchored the long beam, build the other three, cutting them to exact length and bracing them together to form a single U-shaped piece. Raise the assembly into place, and support it.

Use plumb bobs to position the concrete footings. Dig the holes, insert tube forms if you'll be using them, and attach the columns to the undersides of the beams so that they extend at least 8 inches into the holes, with at least 12 inches of concrete under the column. (See "Hanging the Columns," page 48.) Recheck for level, pour the footings, and allow the concrete to set. Do not remove the temporary bracing until the deck is finished.

Bracing and Supporting the Beams

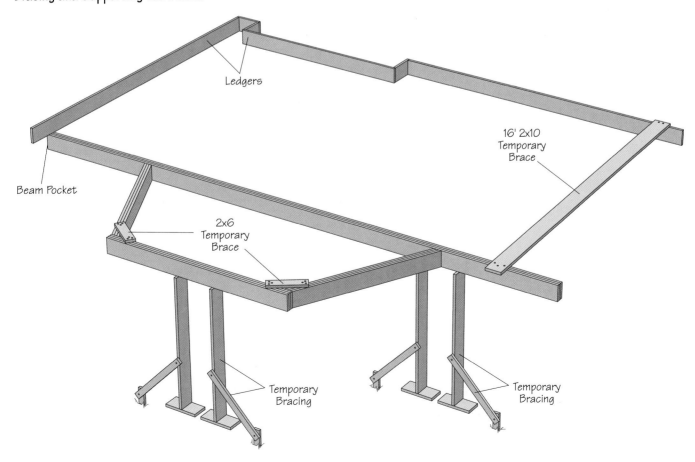

Ledgers

16' 2x10
Temporary
Brace

Beam Pocket

2x6
Temporary
Brace

Temporary
Bracing

Temporary
Bracing

Framing for a Curved Section

After installing the beams, let the joists run wild at the curved section. Mark them for cutting only after you've secured all of them in place. You'll laminate the header for the curved section, which also serves as a fascia, from the same resawn $5/16$-inch thicknesses you use to make the curved bench members described earlier (page 53).

To lay out for the joists, start in the middle. Establish the joist where the tip of the V-shape in the decking will fall. Next, measure 16 inches on center to either side of this joist. Install the joists using joist hangers secured to the ledger. Install the two short header joists, allowing them to run longer than needed. For the curve, splice the joists over the beam, and allow them to run wild past where they will be cut. Double the thickness of the center joist by scabbing on pieces of 2x4. Make sure that you attach the joists firmly in place.

Mark the Curve. To mark the joists for the curve, make a beam compass. To do this, drill two holes exactly 8

Marking Joists for the Curve

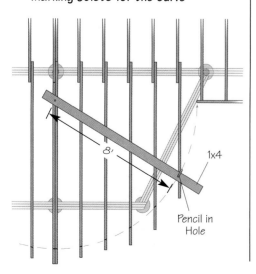

8'

1x4

Pencil in Hole

feet apart in a 10-foot length of 1x4. Use a $3/16$-inch bit for one hole and a $1/4$-inch bit for the other. To establish the centerpoint of the radius, tack a nail through the smaller hole and into the center of the doubled-up joist. Jam a pencil into the other hole, and then swing your compass around the arc to mark the top of each joist.

Use a square to mark plumb lines down from the compass marks, and cut each joist with a circular saw. **Note:** Adjust the bevel of the saw for each cut to make sure that it follows the compass mark on top of the joist.

Curved Fascia. To make the curved header/fascia, resaw 14-foot 2x4s into $5/16$ x $3 1/2$ inch pieces as you did for the laminated bench members. Bend the pieces in place, and fasten them to the ends of the joists. Once you've stacked four of these thicknesses on top of one another, you'll have a strong laminated fascia/header.

Header Detail

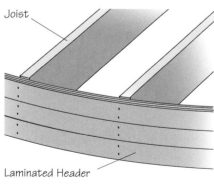

Joist

Laminated Header

Stairway with Landings

A stairway this complicated takes precise figuring and a fair amount of work, but none of the individual operations exceeds the grasp of a do-it-yourselfer. Take the time to check and recheck your layout so that all

steps will have the same rise (vertical height) and run (horizontal length). Once you've installed the footings and framing for the landings, you'll make stringers and treads much as you would for a conventional stairway.

Your deck will probably not have the same height as this one, so use these directions as guidelines. For complete instructions on figuring and installing stairs, see chapter 10 of *Decks: Plan, Design, Build* (as described on page 7 of this book.)

Begin your calculation by figuring the total rise—the distance from the ground at the point where the steps will end to the top of the deck. On a sloped site, estimate where this point will be. (If after doing the calculations you find that the landing will be significantly lower or higher than you estimated, you'll have to figure it out again.) Divide that number by the step height to obtain the number of steps you want. For instance, if your total rise is 86 inches, you can have 12 steps of $7 1/8$ inches each. **Note:** Make sure that all steps have the same rise, or walking up the stairway will feel awkward. Try to keep the step height between 6 and $7 1/2$ inches.

Landings. As you lay out and build, count each landing as a step, and remember that the last step is the ground. Build each landing at the correct height then build the stairs between the landings. For example, the deck surface of the first landing, which is three steps down, should measure $21 3/8$ inches lower than the main deck ($7 1/8$ x 3 = $21 3/8$). The second landing, which is another three steps down, should measure $21 3/8$ inches lower than the top landing and $42 3/4$ inches lower than the top of the deck.

Use the same techniques to build the landings as those you used for the deck. Attach ledgers wherever possible, temporarily supporting the frame at the correct height, and extend posts into the footings. Join the landings to one another using stairs made from three notched carriages. When you've finished the stairs, you'll add the skirting. You will need to attach cleats (2x4 scraps) to the posts to provide a nailing surface for the 1x6 pieces.

Making a Herringbone Decking Pattern

To install the V-shape decking, begin with two long, straight boards near the middle of the deck. (To check them for straightness, stretch a string line along one edge.) Butt-join them, and check for squareness. To do this, mark a line at 9 feet from the end of one board and 12 feet from the end of the other. Adjust the two boards until the distance between the two marks measures 15 feet. (See below.)

Install the rest of the decking using standard spacing, and allow the boards to run wild. Trim the decking so that it overhangs the curved header/fascia by about 1¹/₂ inches.

Butt-Joining Decking

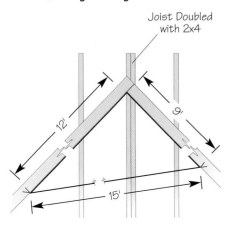

Railing and Stair Handrails

To make the interior posts, use the technique described on page 49. For the corner posts, use three 2x4s and one 1x4, and cut a rabbet in two of the 2x4s as shown by making two passes on the table saw.

Railing and Baluster Elevation

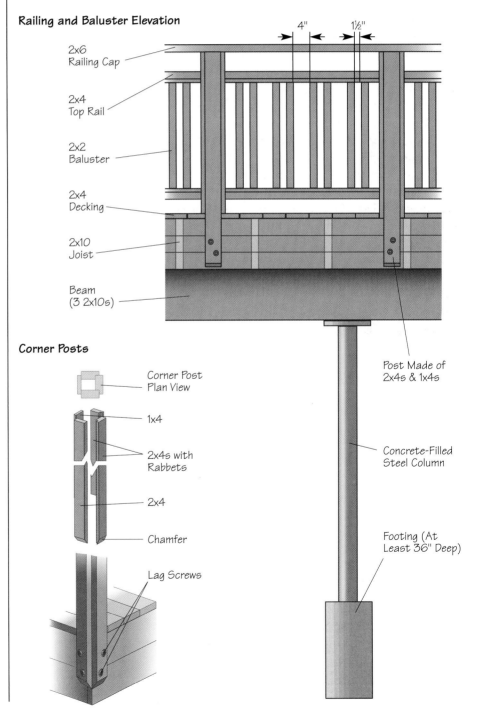

Where a handrail is required for the stairs, make sure that there is enough clearance to grasp it, and anchor it securely. As the drawing on page 53 shows, Kiefer's design (also used on this deck) is fairly simple. Choose clear lumber, sand it smooth, and drill pilot holes for all screws to avoid splitting the small pieces.

Front Porch/Deck for a Corner Lot

*T*hese homeowners wanted a deck with a spa, but they had a corner lot with no true backyard. Kiefer designed a structure that serves as an entry porch on one side and a deck on the other. A striking curved overhead structure adds elegance.

Design Considerations

Those who own corner lots can feel like second-class citizens, because they often have little or no private yard space to call their own. One solution is to build a tall fence, but that can seem unfriendly to the neighbors and make the owners feel claustrophobic. A deck with a substantial railing or trellis can provide some privacy without making it look as though you're trying to shut out the world.

As part of his solution for these homeowners, Kiefer simply treated the rear of the house as a backyard by placing a spa there. A railing with an attention-grabbing overhead structure provides a subtle barrier. The wide expanse of deck space, with its lawn furniture and potted plants, further screens off the spa area and makes it feel more like a deck than a front porch.

Part of the deck serves as an entryway. Just outside the sliding glass doors, a curved landing one step up from the main surface mirrors the larger curve of the deck. A short section of railing, two planters, and an angled bench form an ensemble that nicely frames the entrance into the house.

Two sets of steps that provide access to the lawn incorporate substantial landings. These set off the deck as a private space belonging to the house much more effectively than simple stairways would.

The overhead structure, made of laminated curved pieces and winglike rafters, is a stunning achievement. It contributes more visual appeal than it does shade, and it looks even more inviting with clematis or wisteria climbing up it.

Ground View

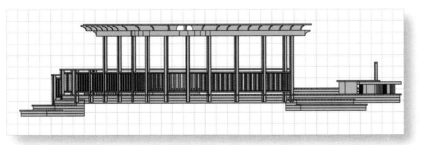

Front Porch/Deck for a Corner Lot, Plan View

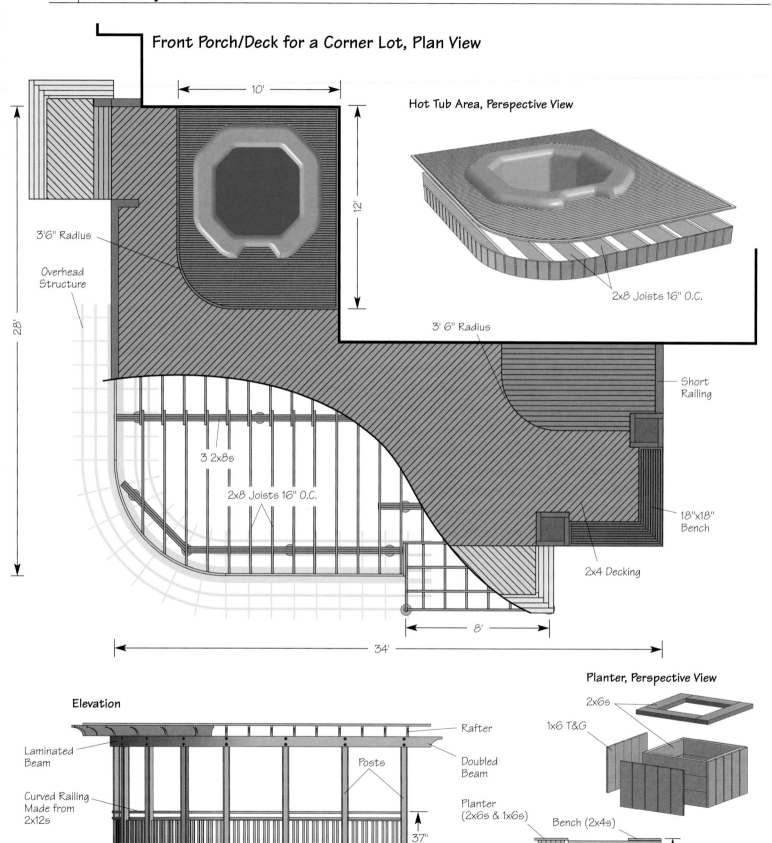

10'

Hot Tub Area, Perspective View

3'6" Radius

Overhead
Structure

28'

12'

2x8 Joists 16" O.C.

3' 6" Radius

Short
Railing

3 2x8s

2x8 Joists 16" O.C.

18"x18"
Bench

2x4 Decking

8'

34'

Planter, Perspective View

2x6s

1x6 T&G

Elevation

Rafter

Laminated
Beam

Posts

Doubled
Beam

Curved Railing
Made from
2x12s

Planter
(2x6s & 1x6s)

Bench (2x4s)

37'

Laminated
Fascia

18"

2x4 Fascia

Concrete Tube Form

Materials Used for This Deck

Framing	Tripled 2x8s for beams 2x8 joists 2x8 ledger pieces and headers	Benches	2x4s for posts 2x4 seat pieces
Decking	2x4s	Planters	2x6 framing pieces 2x6 floor pieces 1x6 tongue-and-groove sides 2x6 top trim
Fascia	2x4s; curved pieces are resawn to ⁵/₁₆" thickness and laminated		
Railing	2x4 post pieces 1x4 post pieces 2x12s for curved top and bottom rails 2x4 straight top and bottom rails 1x2 nailers 2x2 balusters	Hardware	Concrete-filled metal columns Lag screws and washers for ledgers Joist hangers for 2x10s Angle brackets Fasteners for joist hangers 3" deck screws or 10d spiral-shank galvanized nails $1/2$" x $3^1/2$" lag screws with washers, for posts
Overhead	(Posts shared with railing) 2x8 doubled beams; resawn as above 2x8 rafters 2x3 top pieces; resawn as above	Masonry	Concrete Concrete tube forms

Construction Techniques

Use Lally columns set in concrete to support beams made from three 2x8s. (See page 48 for a description of this technique. For framing curves, see page 58.) To support the spa, Kiefer pours a steel-reinforced concrete pad. However, check with your local building department for code requirements.

Planters. To build the bench, see page 53. The planters, though simple in design, must be built carefully using dry, straight lumber.

First, build a simple box from pressure-treated 2x6s laid on edge. For the floor, use 2x6s as well, but lay them flat, and allow ³/₁₆-inch gaps between the boards for drainage. Cover the box with 1x6 tongue-and-groove redwood, and cap it off with 2x6 pieces. Kiefer butt-joins these

rather than mitering them. (See drawing, left.)

Fill the planter with 6 inches of gravel and a couple of inches of sand to ensure that it will drain easily and that the inside boards will have a chance to dry out.

Curved Overhead. This structure resembles an elevated train track. Make winglike end cuts on both the beams and rafters, using the same pattern for each. For the curved beam sections and top pieces, use the laminating technique described on page 53.

Curved Overhead

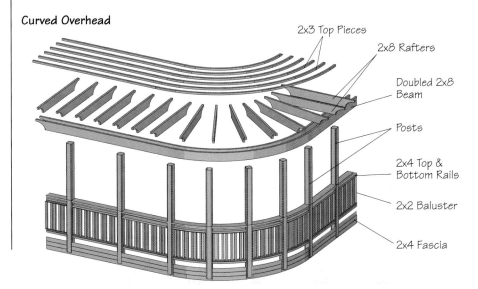

2x3 Top Pieces
2x8 Rafters
Doubled 2x8 Beam
Posts
2x4 Top & Bottom Rails
2x2 Baluster
2x4 Fascia

Veranda with Turned Balusters

he homeowners needed a front porch, but they wanted more than just a structure for entering and exiting the house. By making the porch fairly large and adding a couple of distinctive flourishes, they ended up with a cheery yet classic-looking veranda.

Ground View

Design Considerations

A backyard makes a good place for a showy deck with interesting curves, angles, and levels, but a complicated structure on the front of the house looks out of place. This more public area calls for a more subdued design.

On the other hand, the standard front porch, with its small landing and set of stairs, can look pretty drab. And though you probably wouldn't want to sunbathe, dine, or lounge on a front porch, you might want to sit in a chair and read the paper, pausing to wave to the neighbors from time to time.

This combination porch-deck recalls verandas of the Old South. It can make your neighborhood a slightly friendlier place without putting you entirely on display. The railing partially screens a person sitting in a chair.

Constructed of cedar, the veranda has a slightly less formal look than redwood. Unfortunately, most of the cedar sold today is light-colored sapwood, which doesn't offer a great deal of rot resistance. To compensate for this, apply an annual coat of preservative-sealer.

The design, which could hardly be simpler, consists of a rectangle with a set of stairs. Several details, however, give it a distinctive look. Kiefer designed and built one-of-a-kind newels for the post tops, but the store-bought turned balusters add classic elegance without requiring custom work. The fascia, made from two 2x4s and one 1x4, adds depth to Kiefer's usual banded look.

Veranda with Turned Balusters, Plan View

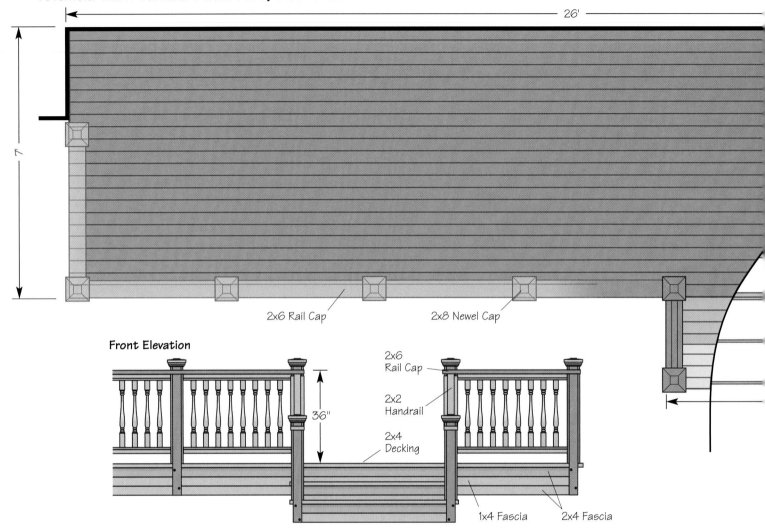

26'

7'

2x6 Rail Cap

2x8 Newel Cap

Front Elevation

2x6
Rail Cap

2x2
Handrail

2x4
Decking

36"

1x4 Fascia

2x4 Fascia

Materials Used for This Deck			
Framing	Tripled 2x8s for beams 2x8 joists 2x8 ledger pieces and headers	Hardware	Concrete-filled metal columns, primed, with screws for attaching to beams Lag screws and washers for installing ledgers
Decking	2x4s		Joist hangers for 2x8s Angle brackets
Fascia	2x4s and 1x4s		Fasteners for joist hangers 3" deck screws or 10d spiral-shank galvanized nails
Railing	2x4 post pieces 1x4 post pieces 2x4 top and bottom rails 1x3 nailers Turned balusters 2x8s and 2x2s for newel pieces 2x6 railing cap 2x2 handrails		$1/2$" x $3^1/2$" lag screws with washers for posts
		Masonry	Concrete Concrete tube forms

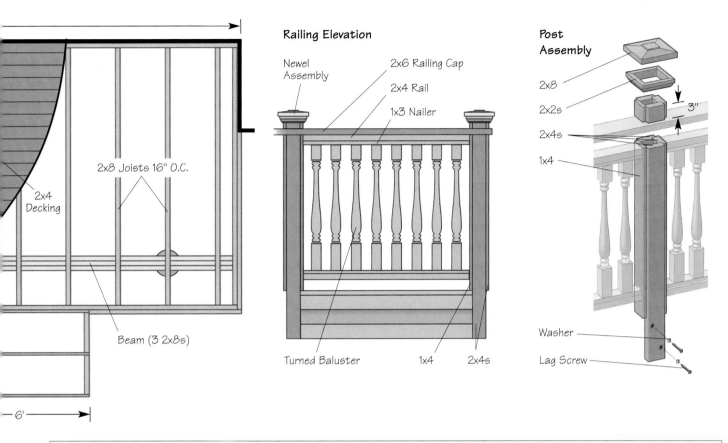

Railing Elevation

Newel Assembly
2x6 Railing Cap
2x4 Rail
1x3 Nailer
Turned Baluster
1x4
2x4s

Post Assembly

2x8
2x2s
2x4s
1x4
3"
Washer
Lag Screw

2x8 Joists 16" O.C.
2x4 Decking
Beam (3 2x8s)
6'

Construction Techniques

This elegant but simple structure goes together fairly quickly. A ledger and a beam, made from three 2x8s and supported by Lally columns, support a simple framing box made from 2x8 joists. Build and attach the posts; then construct the balustrades to fit between them. For descriptions of these techniques, see pages 48–49.

Making the Newels

Attach the railing cap to the tops of the posts. (The posts do not really come up through the cap as they appear to do.) Next, assemble 3-inch versions of the post, drilling pilot holes for the screws to avoid splitting the short pieces. Attach these miniposts to the railing cap, centering them on the posts, by drilling counterbored pilot holes and driving screws down through the 2x4s and into the cap.

You can simply purchase post caps, but you may not get the exact look or material you want. So consider spending a few hours making your own. You can experiment, using a table saw and router, until you come up with the profile that works for you.

This newel is made up from a post cap and trim pieces. To make the cap, measure the actual width of your 2x8 stock (most likely 7¼ inches); then cut a piece to a length that forms a perfect square. Next, move your table-saw fence to the side of the blade opposite its direction of tilt. Set the blade to cut about 3 inches deep, and

then tilt it to 10 degrees from vertical. For safety, attach the cap temporarily to a scrap 2-foot length of 2x8 or 1x8, and then stand this assembly on edge against the table-saw fence. Adjust the fence so that blade will cut away about half (³/₄ inch) of the cap's thickness. Make the first pass to bevel one edge of the cap; then turn the 1x8 carrier board over and bevel the second edge. Now, rotate the cap 90 degrees, reattach it to the carrier board, and repeat to bevel the third and fourth edges.

To make the trim, start with 2- or 3-foot lengths of 2x2 stock, and use a table-mounted router. Cut two ¹/₂-inch coves using a cove bit, and then hand-sand the stock. Miter the pieces to length to fit the posts.

Rambler with Metal Railing

*A*s with "Tilted Square," Kiefer here employs the basic shape of a square. For this design, however, he works with several squares to achieve a deck with a rambling feel. The stainless-steel-tubing railing gives it an open, contemporary look.

Ground View

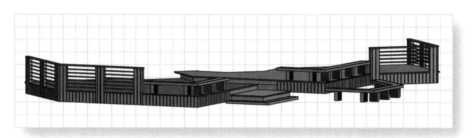

Design Considerations

When it comes to deck shapes, Kiefer believes that simpler is better. However, if you stand on this deck, you aren't conscious of its simplicity. It consists of two large, overlapping squares set at an angle to the house plus a third, smaller one set parallel to the house. Despite the combination of shapes and angles, Kiefer's design conveys a sense of orderliness.

This deck provides three distinct usable areas that flow together to produce a relaxed, informal feel. Off the sliding door, a cooking site stands apart from the other areas. In the center, a larger space can accommodate a table with chairs and is easily reached from the kitchen. At the opposite end, the largest area offers ample room for lounging and entertaining. A three-sided bench protrudes into the yard from the middle area, giving it an even more expansive feel. The deck is set on a ground-level patio surface, so a nice touch is that the bench encloses a small area for plants, making the deck feel closer to the yard.

The unusual railing incorporates stainless-steel horizontal rails and solid redwood vertical sections. **Note:** It's possible for young children to climb this style of railing, so the local building department may not approve it. Check codes in your area before you proceed. In this setting, the railing has a more decorative than practical function because the deck surface measures less than 24 inches above ground level.

Rambler with Metal Railing, Plan View

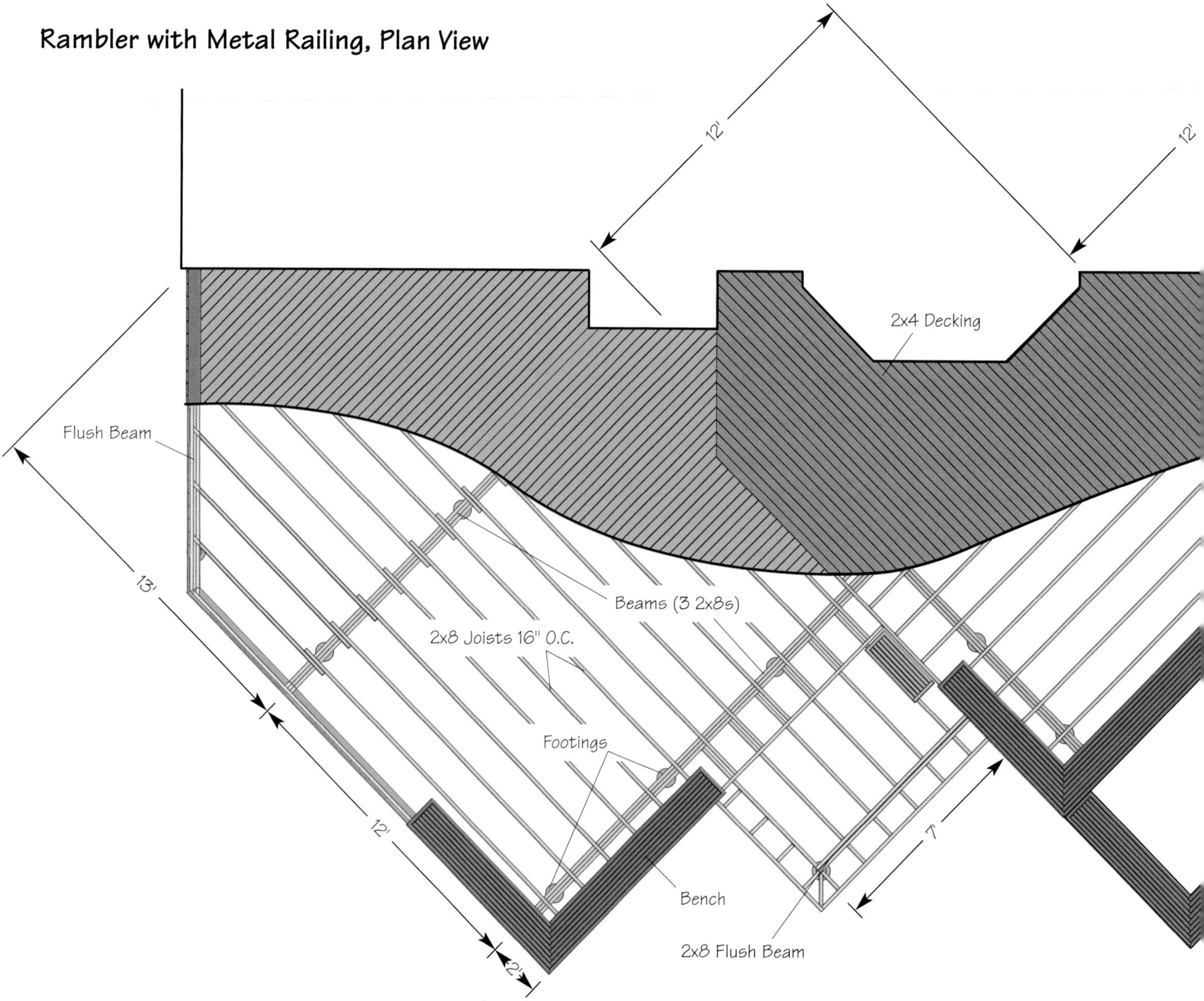

12'

12'

2x4 Decking

Flush Beam

13'

Beams (3 2x8s)

2x8 Joists 16" O.C.

Footings

12'

7'

Bench

2'

2x8 Flush Beam

Step Framing Detail

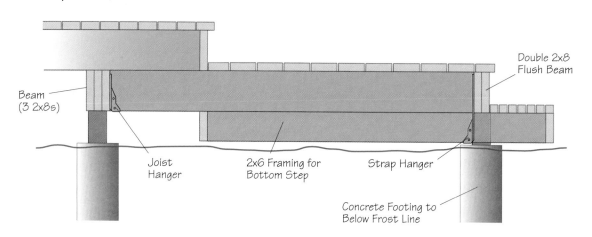

Double 2x8
Flush Beam

Beam
(3 2x8s)

Joist
Hanger

2x6 Framing for
Bottom Step

Strap Hanger

Concrete Footing to
Below Frost Line

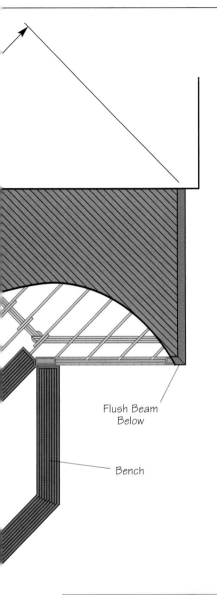

Flush Beam
Below

Bench

Construction Techniques

To begin framing, use beam pockets and Lally columns as described on page 48.

Note the various heights of the beams. Remember that a "flush beam" is set at the same height as the joists. The joists attach to the beam with joist hangers rather than sitting on top of it. The three non-flush beams for the raised level measure $7^{1}/4$ inches higher than the non-flush beams. At one point, one of the upper-level beams rests on a lower-level beam. Don't set up the short beam for the lower landing yet— wait until you've completed the framing for the main deck.

Ledger Layout

Laying out the ledger at the points where joists attach to it diagonally is tricky. Fortunately, most of these joists split on a beam and need not be cut accurately to length. On these ledgers, the marks for the joists will measure $22^{1}/2$ inches on center. You may want to draw lines and install the joists in the usual way, using $22^{1}/2$ inches instead of 16 inches. You may, however, find it best to lay out the joists in an as-you-go fashion. To use this approach, cut one end of each joist at 45 degrees. Set up one of the joists in the middle of the run, and check to make sure that it sits at a 45-degree angle to the house. To do

Split Joists

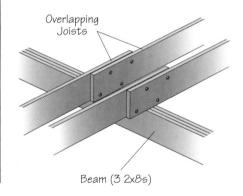

Overlapping
Joists

Beam (3 2x8s)

Materials Used for This Deck

Framing	Tripled 2x8s for beams 2x8 joists 2x8 ledgers and headers 2x6 stair framing pieces	Hardware	Concrete-filled metal columns, primed, with screws for attaching to beams $1^{1}/4$"-dia. 18-ga. stainless-steel tubing for railing Holding brackets 3" deck screws or 10d spiral-shank galvanized nails Fasteners for joist hangers Joist hangers for 2x8s Angled joist hangers for 2x8s Angle brackets Lag screws with washers for anchoring the ledger
Decking	2x4s		
Railing & Fascia	1x6s, tongue-and-groove 2x4 framing pieces 2x6 railing caps 1x4 fascia pieces 2x4 edging for bottom step		
Benches	2x6 legs 2x2 seat pieces 2x4 edging	Masonry	Concrete Concrete tube forms

this, make a mark exactly 20 feet along the length of this joist, and another that measures 168½ inches along the ledger. Adjust the joist until a measuring tape held perpendicular to it indicates 168½ inches from the mark on the ledger to the mark on the joist.

To make sure that the rest of the joists are properly spaced, use 14½-inch lengths of 2x8. Stretch a string line to verify that the pairs of joists that split on a beam run in straight lines.

Railing with Steel Tubes. You may have trouble finding the stainless-steel tubing. If your building center cannot supply them for you, try sheet-metal specialists. First, build the extra-wide rail posts from pressure-treated 2x4s and 1x6 tongue-

and-groove redwood. On the two sides, allow one edge of the 1x6 to overlap and conceal the outside joists, thus making the upper part of the fascia. You'll need to use precision in laying out the holes for the steel tubes where they insert into the framing before cutting or drilling.

Construct the frames for the railing posts from 2x4s, tying the uprights into the framing as shown. Using a hole saw, drill 1¼-inch holes through the pieces that will accept the steel tubing, spacing them 5 inches on center. Set the frames in place on the decking. Trim the decking boards to size before fastening the railing posts in place.

Cut the steel tubing to lengths that fit snugly against the rear 2x4 framing

pieces (the ones without holes). Assemble the tubes and frames together; then fasten the post frames to the deck by driving long screws into the decking and bolts into the joists. **Note:** Drill pilot holes to avoid splitting the short 2x4 plates.

Clad the post frames with 1x6 tongue-and-groove redwood. The fascia pieces should extend 5 inches below the joist. Fill in all the fascia pieces, ripping these pieces to width as necessary. However, if you'll need room to crawl under the deck to fasten the bench legs, you may want to build the benches before installing the fascia. (See the following text.)

Building the Benches

You'll build and attach the benches after installing the decking. Use 2x6s and spacers for the upright supports, and make the seat sections to fit between the railing posts.

Using a table saw, resaw redwood stock to a thickness of 5/16 inch for the spacers. Cut this material to 1 x 2½ inches for the seats and 1½ x 4 inches for the legs. **Note:** Make sure that all spacers are identical in thickness.

For each leg, cut seven 15½-inch lengths of 2x6 for a bench that measures 17 inches high. Sandwich two spacers between the 2x6s, and then fasten the assembly using deck screws. **Note:** Do not drive the screws through the spacers, or they could split. At the upper end of each assembled leg, fasten a spacer for the edging piece.

Attach the legs to the deck. If possible, drive screws up through the decking. If you can't, carefully drill pilot holes and attach the legs from above using

Laying Out the First Angled Joist

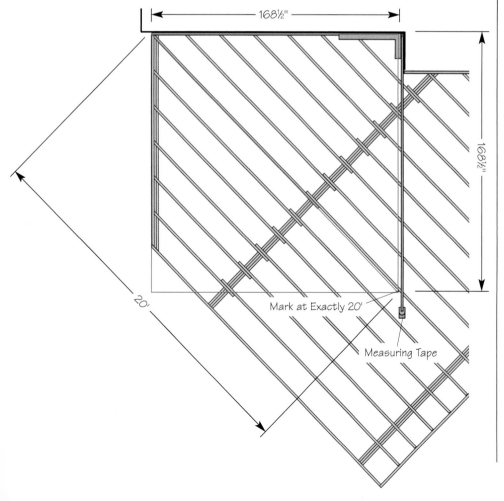

168½"

168½"

20'

Mark at Exactly 20'

Measuring Tape

Railing and Post Construction

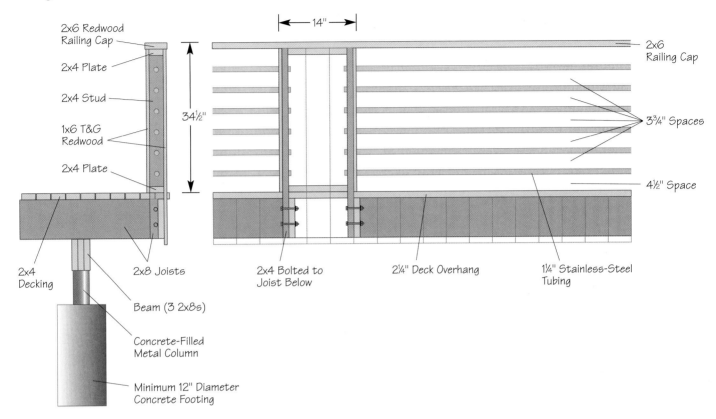

2x6 Redwood Railing Cap

2x4 Plate

2x4 Stud

1x6 T&G Redwood

2x4 Plate

34½"

2x4 Decking

2x8 Joists

Beam (3 2x8s)

Concrete-Filled Metal Column

Minimum 12" Diameter Concrete Footing

14"

2x6 Railing Cap

3¾" Spaces

4½" Space

2x4 Bolted to Joist Below

2¼" Deck Overhang

1¼" Stainless-Steel Tubing

angle-driven screws. To secure the bench to a patio surface, use angle irons and lag screws with shields.

Miter the ends of the long 2x4 edging pieces; then attach them to the legs with deck screws so that they protrude upward 1½ inches. Next, miter the shorter edging pieces and attach them to the long pieces, using casing nails. Where the bench meets a railing post, attach the edging firmly to the post.

Fill in the seat sections with the 2x2s. To do this, first cut the seat pieces slightly longer than needed. On a flat surface, sandwich them together using the spacers as shown. Again, do not drive screws through the spacers. Lay the assembled seat sections in place; then mark and cut them to length. Slip them in, and attach them to the edging.

Bench Construction

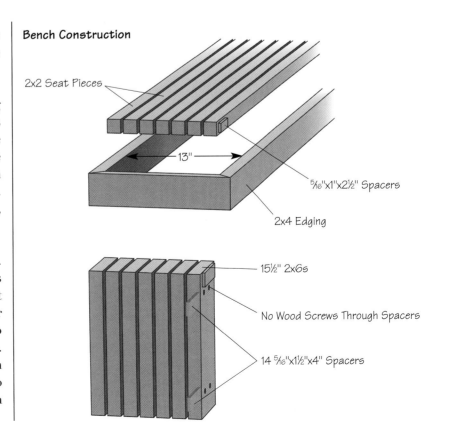

2x2 Seat Pieces

13"

⁵⁄₁₆"x1"x2½" Spacers

2x4 Edging

15½" 2x6s

No Wood Screws Through Spacers

14 ⁵⁄₁₆"x1½"x4" Spacers

George Drummond
Casa Decks
Virginia Beach, Virginia
(757) 523-4505
www.casadecks.com

George Drummond of Casa Decks in Virginia Beach, Virginia, has a knack for building modestly priced decks that have plenty of flair and tailored features. Though the majority of Drummond's decks are on the small side, they never seem to feel cramped. He manages to use space efficiently and eliminate traffic bottlenecks by allotting just the right amount of room for all the things people usually do on a deck.

Design Considerations

Before Drummond designs a deck, he asks the homeowners what they intend to use it for. He then maps out a plan that will allow them to do those things comfortably. In his experience, most families feel comfortable with the smaller-scale parameters he's developed. Once they establish the overall dimensions, he helps the clients develop a look for their deck.

Sizing a Deck

In his experience, Drummond has found that the following dimensions suit most families.

■ For a dining area, a 10x10-foot space will suffice as a bare minimum; 12x12 feet usually works better. This allows room for a round or square table, six chairs, and enough clearance to get in and out of the seats.

■ A cooking area should measure at least 5x8 feet. This provides space for

▲ *Drummond sometimes changes decking orientation to add interest without dramatically adding to the cost of the deck.*

▶ *An excellent example of Drummond's work, this deck, with its beautiful railing, overhead structure, and gazebo, fits the architectural style of suburban Virginia.*

a gas or charcoal grill, two or three people standing near it, and a small table to hold the meat and sauce. If room for more elaborate food preparation is required, Drummond frequently adds a counter-type table and enough space for a person to work at it, which typically increases the total area to 5x11 feet.

■ A lounge chair requires a 5x8-foot space, including room for setting drinks and getting in and out.

■ An average spa or whirlpool takes up a 10x10-foot space. This allows for a $7^1/_2$x$7^1/_2$-foot spa, a seating area, and a place to stow the cover.

■ Traffic paths should measure approximately 4 feet wide, and they should provide access to all functional areas.

Adding Interest

Because Drummond's clients usually want a modestly priced deck, they often assume they'll have to settle for a plain, boxy rectangular structure. But Drummond avoids the "tacked-on" look of decks that typically come with new homes. Drawing on his considerable experience, he manages to add interesting angles and turns without adding much to the price. In his view, there's no reason why even the least expensive deck shouldn't have an interesting focal point.

Drummond uses a computer-assisted-design (CAD) program to generate precise drawings for every deck project. That way, his clients

▲ **Sometimes just clipping a corner** *changes the deck enough to enhance its visual interest.*

◄ **Numerous decking options** *are available, including plastic materials. Wood-polymer decking is shown here.*

have no questions about the number or dimensions of the structural pieces. A CAD drawing also gives them a clear idea of what their deck will look like.

Although Drummond would rather build a greater variety of deck designs, he usually finds that his clients want him to stick with the tried-and-true. They tend to look through his portfolio and select a design he's already built rather than give him the go-ahead to come up with new ideas. To try to overcome this tendency to go with a sure thing, Drummond reminds them that they may lose out on the possibility of getting something truly unique.

Lumber. On most of his decks, Drummond uses pressure-treated Southern yellow pine for all elements. This material costs a good deal less than cedar or redwood, but he selects it with care to get the best possible pieces. Lesser grades often splinter and sometimes don't have adequate treatment in them to prevent rot, so he must be careful.

Drummond's clients find that by staining pressure-treated pine every year or two, they can keep it looking like a more-expensive wood such as cedar or redwood. In fact, a deck doesn't usually look its best until after the second staining. With many of Drummond's decks, one would be hard pressed to tell whether they are treated pine, cedar, or redwood. A few clients finish their decks with a solid-color stain. In these cases, the lower cost of the treated lumber makes it the clear choice.

▲ *A diagonal herringbone-pattern skirt gives an ordinary deck visual interest.*

▶ *Note the counter on this deck, which makes good practical use of the pergola's post.*

Techniques to Use

▶ Whenever a deck calls for steps, Drummond likes to make them at least 14 inches deep. Although 11 to 12 inches is considered the standard tread depth for a stairway, this dimension in his view doesn't "feel right" on a deck. Drummond believes that standard-depth treads pose a tripping hazard, because people expect deck dimensions to be more relaxed and expansive than those on a regular stairway.

▶ Although pressure-treated pine is generally held to be of lower quality than redwood or cedar, it offers superior resistance to rot, dents, and scratches. And, of course, it costs less. As Drummond's decks show, if you choose the boards carefully and stain them, treated lumber can rival redwood for comfort and appearance.

▶ For the decking, railing, and other visible elements, Drummond pays extra to get No. 1 lumber. This grade is less likely to shrink and crack, which ensures a better-looking deck over the long term and fewer splinters. It also has fewer knots and tends to be straighter.

▶ Drummond's approach—planning for functional areas and traffic paths—makes it easier to maximize your possibilities with limited resources. But even if you're building a large deck with expensive materials, make sure you allot space carefully for each functional area, or you may end up with lots of unusable space.

▶ For the structural members, Drummond pays less but still chooses carefully. He uses "No. 2 or better," which most building departments require, but he selects old-growth lumber. In most parts of the country, pine will offer better quality than "hem-fir," a general designation that includes wood that sometimes shrinks and warps severely. (In some regions, hem-fir may perform well, but check with people who have used it.)

▶ Drummond allows his lumber more ground contact than most builders—many of his skirts extend below lawn level—but he takes precautions to ensure that it can handle the moisture. Although some companies produce treated lumber with chromated copper arsenate (CCA) retention levels as low as 0.25 (liters of chemical per cubic foot), Drummond never uses lumber with a CCA retention level of less than 0.40. In cases where structural pieces actually sit in soil that may be moist for much of the year, he selects lumber with a 0.60 CCA retention (more than ½ pound per cubic foot). Lumberyards don't generally carry this product, but you can usually special-order it.

▶ Note the counter design on page 85. Instead of mitering the corners of the countertop and bench pieces on the deck, Drummond carries them through, giving the structures a great deal more strength as well as a more interesting appearance. And as most experienced deck builders have discovered, mitered joints tend to pull apart as wood shrinks, leaving unsightly gaps.

▶ When building low to the ground, Drummond places landscape fabric on top of the joists before installing the decking. If you live in an area with lush vegetation as he does, the fabric ensures that you won't have grass growing up through the cracks in the decking.

▶ When building a deck that sits less than 5 feet off the ground, Drummond usually does not attach it to the house with a ledger board. This may add a bit to the up-front materials and labor cost because it requires more footings and posts. But on most decks, Drummond believes that even a flashed ledger may allow moisture to collect, which over the long term can damage both the deck and the house.

▶ Most of Drummond's decks have "solid" skirts that hide the framing and concrete footings. (Actually, there are ⅛- to 1-inch gaps between the vertical or herringbone-patterned skirt pieces.) Although a skirt gives a deck a finished look, some people are reluctant to install one, either because it adds labor and expense or because they worry about cutting off air circulation beneath the deck. However, Drummond has found that a skirt adds little to the overall cost and effort, and that the gaps between the skirt and decking pieces allow adequate circulation, even during the hot, humid summers in Virginia.

▶ *Gray decking contrasts with white-painted railings and trimwork for a refined, elegant look on this deck. (Another view of the deck is shown on page 75.)*

Floating Octagons
with Walkways

R *ather than build a small rectangular deck just off the house for barbecuing and lounging, Drummond and the home-owners came up with this solution, which extends the outdoor living areas farther into the yard. Wooden path-ways lead to octagonal platforms that sit among flower beds and overhanging trees. One octagon serves as a small dining area, and the other contains a bar and refrigerator.*

Ground View

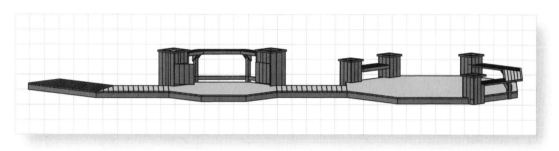

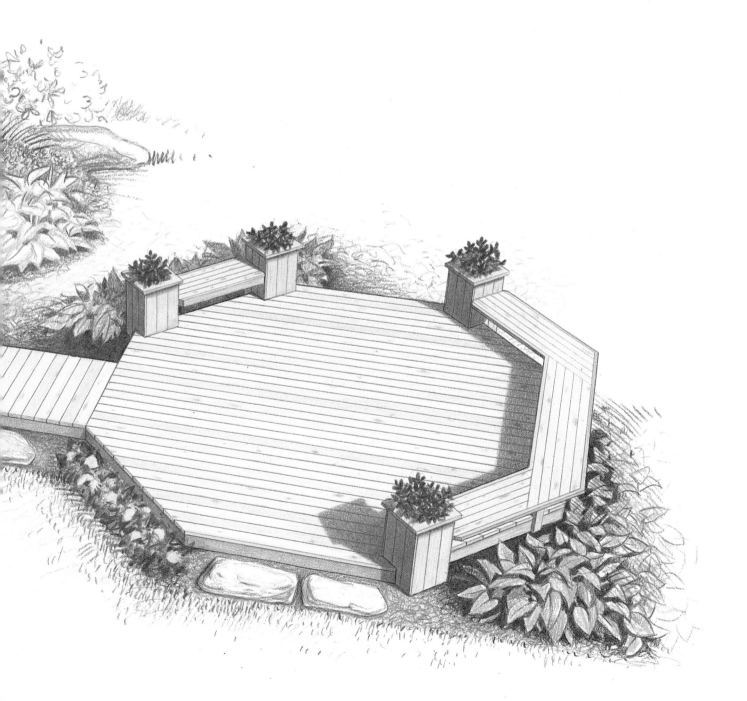

Floating Octagons with Walkways, Plan View

Elevation with Flower Box

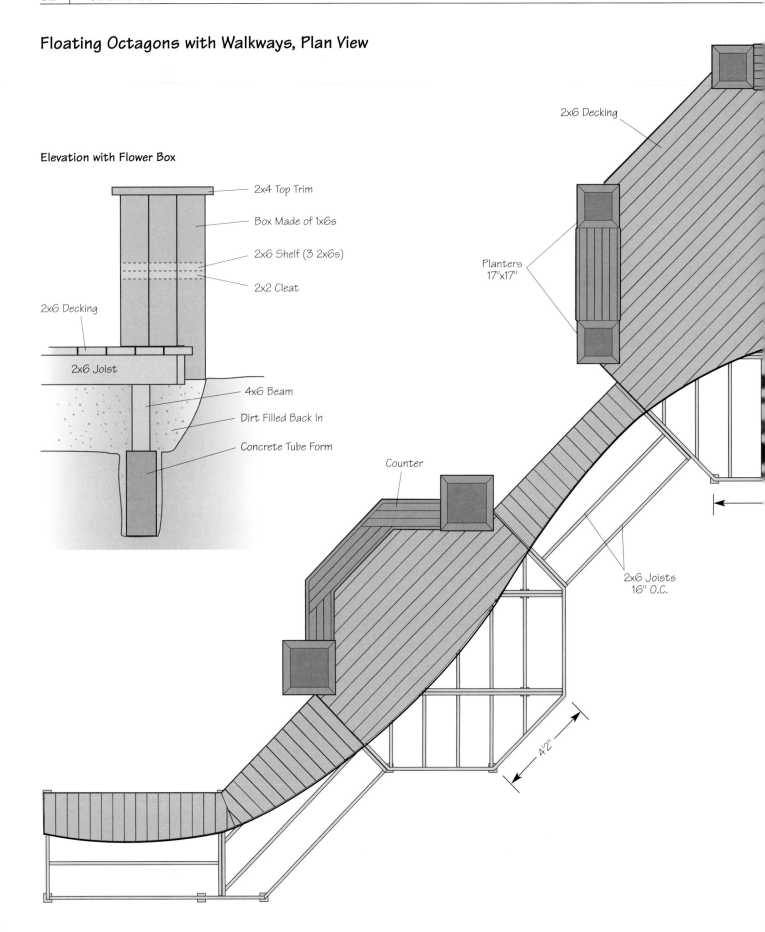

2x4 Top Trim

Box Made of 1x6s

2x6 Shelf (3 2x6s)

2x2 Cleat

2x6 Decking

2x6 Joist

4x6 Beam

Dirt Filled Back In

Concrete Tube Form

2x6 Decking

Planters
17"x17"

Counter

2x6 Joists
16" O.C.

4'2"

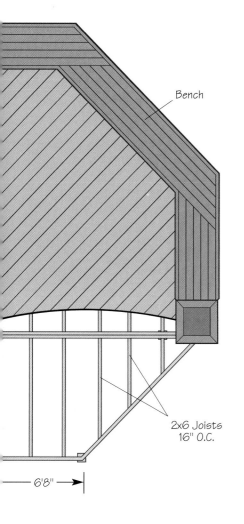

Bench

2x6 Joists
16" O.C.

6'8"

Design Considerations

The surface of this treated-pine complex rises only slightly above ground level, making it more a part of the surroundings than a promontory from which to view the yard. In fact, the octagons and walkways seem almost to "float" in the yard.

That sensation is modified, however, by the built-in bench and counter, which emphasize that this structure is a dining and entertaining center. The smaller octagon offers just enough space for preparing and barbecuing food. The larger octagon easily accommodates a large table and chairs for dining.

Planter Boxes. The benches and counter both incorporate generously sized planter boxes. The boxes contain large pots rather than loose dirt, which allows the homeowners to change plants as they flower. The planters that adjoin the counter house small cabinets underneath. Drummond routed wiring to one of these to provide power for a small refrigerator. This keeps food and drinks cool for when the clients entertain on hot summer days.

Building a deck this close to the ground (especially one with no ledger) requires a lot of digging, so recruit plenty of strong-backed help if you can. A high-school kid or two hired for an afternoon may save your body some serious wear and tear. If the soil in your yard is difficult to excavate, you may want to choose a design that doesn't protrude so far into the ground—for instance, one that calls for 2x8 or even 2x10 joists and flush beams rather than under-joist beams.

Materials Used for This Deck

Framing	4x4 posts 4x6 beams (2 2x6s) 2x6 joists	Planters and Cabinets	1x6 side pieces 2x4 top trim pieces 2x6 shelves 2x2 cleats 15-lb. roofing felt (planter lining)
Decking (approx. 460 sq. ft.)	2x6s		
		Hardware	3" lag screws with washers for bench posts Joist hangers for 2x6s Angled joist hangers for 2x6s Angle brackets Fasteners for joist hangers 2" deck screws 3" deck screws Self-closing hinges for cabinet doors
Benches	4x4 posts 2x4 framing pieces 2x6 seat braces 2x6 seat pieces and edging		
Counter	4x4 posts 2x4 angle braces 2x4 bottom braces 2x4 countertop pieces and edging 2x2 braces for countertop		
		Masonry	Concrete Concrete tube forms

Construction Techniques

Supporting a Deck Nearly Flush to the Ground

Drummond used 0.60 CCA pressure-treated Southern yellow pine. This grade is so saturated with treating agent that Drummond feels comfortable sinking the beams into the ground. Although 0.40 CCA lumber is rated suitable for ground contact, you may want to special-order the higher-rated lumber.

Lay out the corners of the decks and walkways using stakes. Based on the highest point in your yard, establish the desired heights of the decks. String level lines on the stakes, and then excavate to a depth of $7^1/2$ inches below the string lines for the entire deck and $5^1/2$ inches deeper for the beams. Allow yourself plenty of room to work.

Footings. Lay out and dig the footing holes. The smaller deck requires four beam footings (two for each beam) and four perimeter footings. The dining deck has six beam footings (three for each beam) and four perimeter footings.

For the beam footings, position a concrete tube form in each footing hole so that its bottom end measures $12^1/2$ inches below the future surface of your deck. Use a water level, line level, or carpenter's level laid on top of a long, straight board to level the tube forms with one another. Anchor the tube forms firmly with scrap 2x4s and screws, as shown in the detail drawing. For the footings that do not

support beams, set the tube forms $5^1/2$ inches higher than those for the beam footings. **Note:** Before you do this, check the actual width of your 4x6s. If they don't measure exactly $5^1/2$ inches wide, adjust the height of the non-beam footings accordingly.

The local building department may require the use of anchoring hardware for beams that rest on footings. However, such hardware is not really necessary because the 4x6 beams will not wander off the footings once you build the framing. Pour the concrete, and allow it to set.

Framing for Freestanding Octagons

Set the beams in place, but do not cut them to exact length yet. Adjust the baseplate on your circular saw for a $22^1/2$-degree cut (to yield a $67^1/2$-degree bevel on your good piece). Then cut eight 2x6 joists to a length of 80 inches (on the long side) and eight more to 50 inches (also on the long side). Screw together these two sets of outside joists on top of their respective beams. The beam struc-

tures will be a bit flimsy and not yet perfectly square, but they will firm up as you add the joists. The two octagons will measure about 3 inches shy of 10 and 16 feet in diameter, which will allow for the $1^1/2$-inch decking overhang.

On each octagon, measure for the interior joists; then square-cut them to fit. Make sure that all interior joists for each octagon measure exactly the same length. Now, check for squareness. Add the remaining joists, and then build the frames for the pathways. Lay the decking, allowing it to overhang the framing $1^1/2$ inches on all sides.

Planters, Cabinets, and Counter

The flower boxes and storage cabinets should have a simple, rustic appearance, so don't attempt to make them look like fine cabinetry. However, select good-looking wood that is not likely to shrink, warp, or crack. No. 1 pressure-treated lumber that is labeled KDAT (kiln-dried after treatment) makes a good choice.

Establishing Footings That Are Level with Each Other

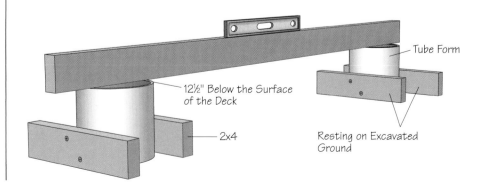

Tube Form

$12^1/2$" Below the Surface of the Deck

2x4

Resting on Excavated Ground

Planters. For each flower box, cut five pieces of tongue-and-groove 1x6 lumber to a length of $22^1/2$ inches, five pieces to $22^1/2$ inches plus the distance you want the front to travel downward to the ground, and two pieces that are notched as shown.

Assemble each side, attaching 2x2 braces at the top and bottom with $2^1/2$-inch deck screws. Check each side for squareness. Notch out the decking overhang for each box. Join the sides together, check the box for squareness, and then cut 2x6 shelf pieces to fit. Attach the shelf and the 2x4 top trim pieces with 3-inch decking screws. Build the benches as described on page 97, but assemble the seat lumber as shown with this deck for a more interesting effect. (See pages 80–82.)

Cabinets. Construct the cabinets in much the same way you did the flower boxes, but make the sides taller. Also, add a second 2x6 shelf at the bottom. Build the side with the door as shown; then make a door that measures 2 inches larger than the opening in both directions. Install self-closing hinges so you won't have to worry about latches.

If, like Drummond's clients, you would like to have a refrigerator, hire an electrician to run an underground cable in conduit that is approved by the local building department. You may need to have a new circuit installed as well.

Counter. Lay the pieces for the counter on the deck, and measure them for cutting. Assemble the counter upside down so that you won't end up with screwheads on the working surface. Lay three 2x4 countertop pieces flat, and then sandwich them between two 2x4 edging pieces laid on edge. Attach 2x2 braces at both ends and every 2 feet or so to keep the top flush with the edging. Then attach the edging to the countertop.

Cut the posts to $34^1/2$ inches long. On the bottom ends, cut out a notch that measures $1^3/4$ inches deep and $8^3/4$ inches long. Install them as you would rail posts. Set the counter on top of the posts and cabinets, level it, and attach it to the cabinets using 2-inch screws. Drive the screws from the inside of the cabinet into the 2x2 braces. Lastly, cut angle braces, and screw them to the posts and the counter from underneath.

Flower Boxes

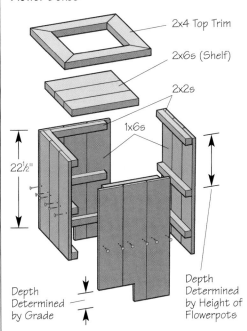

Building the Counter

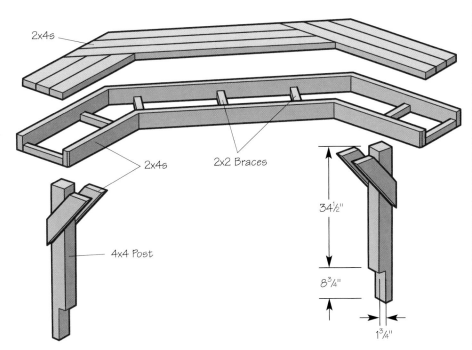

Cabinet with Door

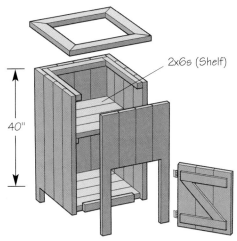

Aboveground Pool Surround

*A*s Drummond's clients discovered, this is a handsome way to dress up an inexpensive aboveground swimming pool. However, be aware that materials and labor for a structure like this can run up some serious expense. If you don't already own an aboveground model, you may find that a standard in-ground pool wouldn't cost appreciably more.

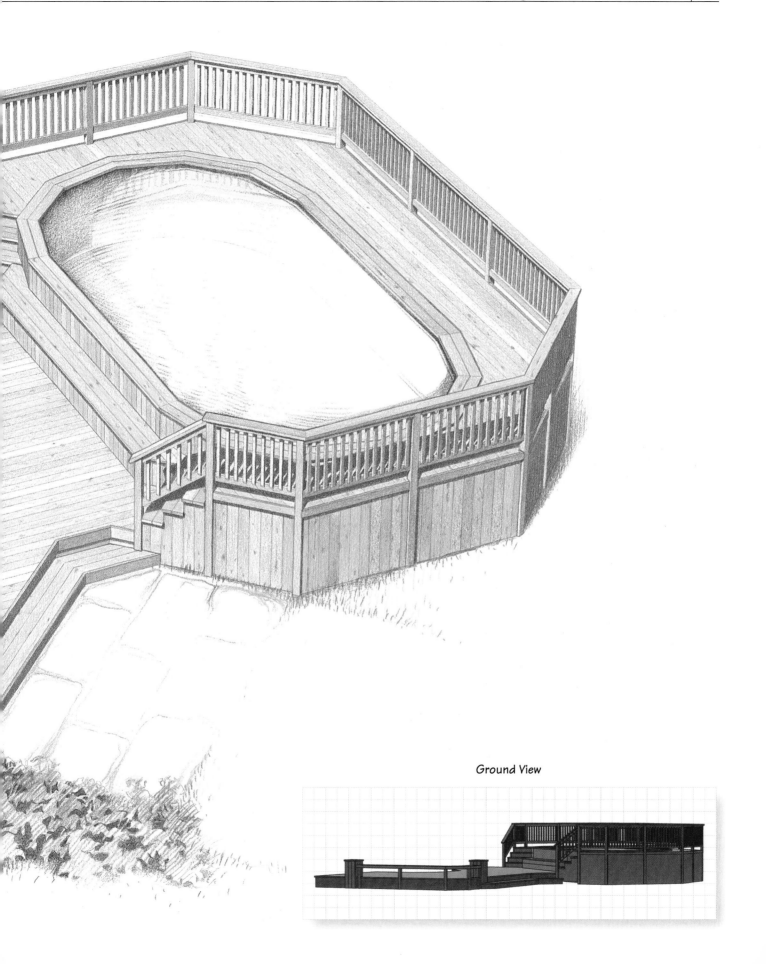

Ground View

Aboveground Pool Surround, Plan View

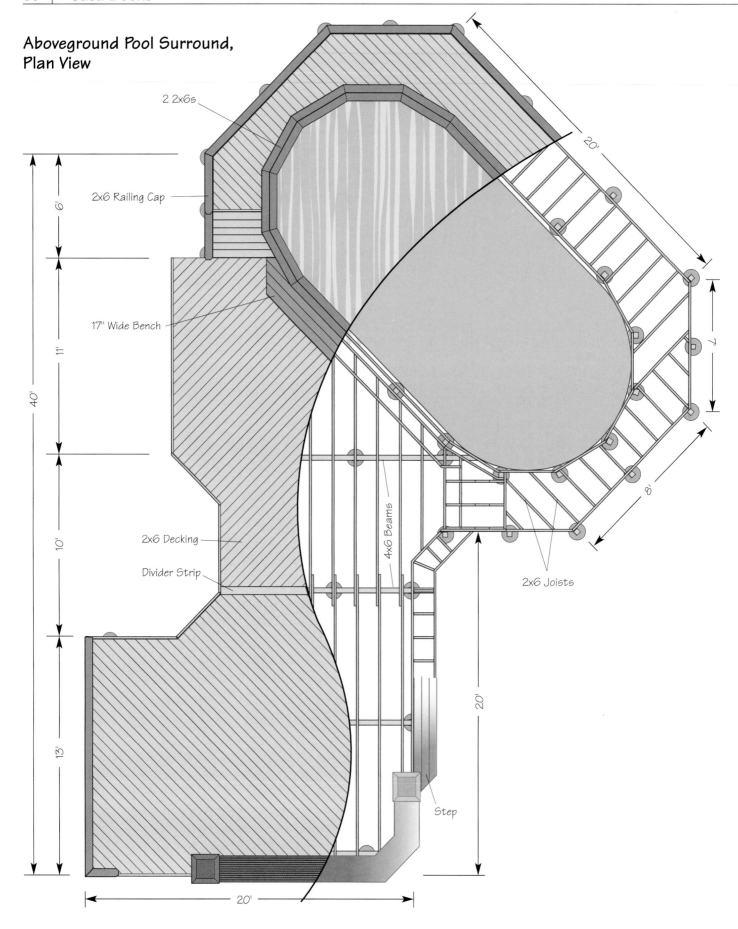

2 2x6s

2x6 Railing Cap

17" Wide Bench

2x6 Decking

Divider Strip

4x6 Beams

2x6 Joists

Step

6'

11'

40'

10'

13'

20'

20'

7'

8'

20'

Design Considerations

The homeowners primarily wanted a smooth transition to the pool. The house occupies a corner lot, which means that setback requirements limited the area that they could use. Still, they wanted something of a rambling feel. Drummond's design allows them to step from a breakfast nook onto a lower deck that provides ample room for dining and lounging, and to move easily from there up to pool level.

Pool Surround. A 4-foot-wide walkway runs around two-thirds of the pool, allowing enough room for swimmers to pull themselves out of the water and sit with their feet dangling in it. This also provides enough width for a lounge chair, provided there isn't much traffic. (If you prefer a full-scale lounging area next to the pool, allow at least 6 feet.) Because there are two walkways leading to this area, traffic rarely poses a problem.

Along the other one-third of the pool, a fixed bench on the lower deck provides a place for buffet eating. The skirting that covers the pool serves as the back for the bench. Around the perimeter of the pool, solid skirting alternates with lattice panels, some of which are hinged to allow access to pool machinery and to provide usable storage space.

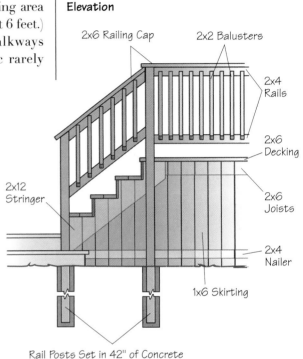

Elevation

2x6 Railing Cap
2x2 Balusters
2x4 Rails
2x6 Decking
2x12 Stringer
2x6 Joists
2x4 Nailer
1x6 Skirting
Rail Posts Set in 42" of Concrete

Materials Used for This Deck

Framing	4x4 posts 4x6s (or doubled 2x6s) for beams 2x6 joists	Planters	2x6 seat pieces and edging 2x4 top cap pieces 2x4 framing pieces 1x6 tongue-and-groove for sides 15-lb. roofing felt for lining
Stairs	2x6s for treads 2x12 stringers 1x8 risers	Hardware	Joist hangers for 2x6s Angled joist hangers for 2x6s Angle brackets Fasteners for joist hangers 3" deck screws or 10d galvanized nails 3" lag screws with washers for rail and bench posts 2½" deck screws for attaching balusters
Decking	2x6s		
Skirt	1x6 verticals 2x4 edging		
Railing	4x4 posts (also used as structural posts) 2x6 railing cap 2x4 top and bottom rails 2x2 balusters		
Benches	4x4 posts 2x4 framing pieces 2x6 seat braces	Masonry	Concrete Concrete tube forms

Construction Techniques

The lower deck calls for standard techniques, but constructing symmetrical, firm framing around the pool for the upper deck poses more of a challenge. In Drummond's design, the posts for this framing carry through upward, so they can double as rail posts.

Building Around a Raised Pool

Pools of this type can be fairly strong, but don't use the pool to support the deck in any way. It isn't built to take this kind of strain. This means that you must build and support the deck so that it doesn't touch the pool or end up bearing on the pool in the future. To ensure this, use spacers that keep all joists and posts at least $3/4$ inch away from the pool edge, and hold the decking off the pool edge by $1/2$ inch or so. Also, install solid footings, and set them well below the frost line for your area.

Footings. The pool surround, a nearly freestanding structure that measures about 6 feet high, needs more lateral support than most decks. The solution is to sink numerous posts deep in the ground and fill each hole with plenty of concrete. This requires lots of deep footing holes, so consider hiring a landscaping company to dig them for you. At the very least, recruit some help and rent a power auger. For the posts, select lumber that has a CCA rating of 0.40 or higher that can withstand ground contact. If you cut off the end that goes into the ground,

soak it in preservative for a while before installing it.

The pool surround does not require beams. Your inspector may insist that you double the outside joists, but positioning the posts every 5 to 6 feet gives the structure plenty of support. The solid skirting adds rigidity. Along the bench-side edge of the pool, joists attached to both sides of the posts provide adequate support for a narrow ledge.

Post Locations. Lay out the post locations next to the pool first. Check your pool sides for plumb; if they aren't, vary your measurements

accordingly. At each end of the pool, locate the exact center of the curve, and dig a posthole at this point, centering it 4 inches from the edge of the pool. Next, dig holes at the points on both sides where the curve begins. Then locate two in-between holes as shown. Center all holes 4 inches from the pool edge.

Lay out and dig the remaining postholes. Make the holes that will hold structural rail posts at least 42 inches deep to provide stiffness. The other holes need only follow local codes for footings. Build the framing before you pour concrete. (See the Plan View, Elevation, and

Pool Post Locations

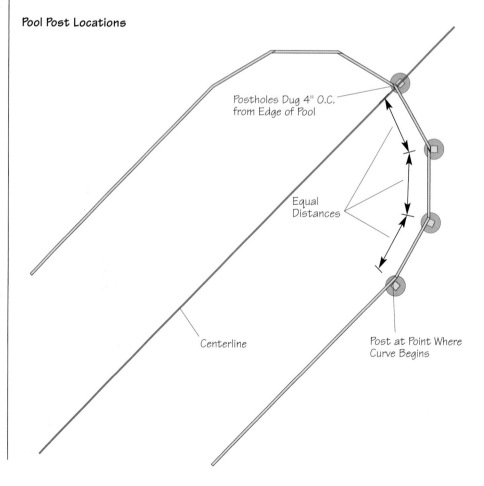

Postholes Dug 4" O.C. from Edge of Pool

Equal Distances

Centerline

Post at Point Where Curve Begins

Framing Detail

Note: Posts Set in Holes—No Concrete Yet

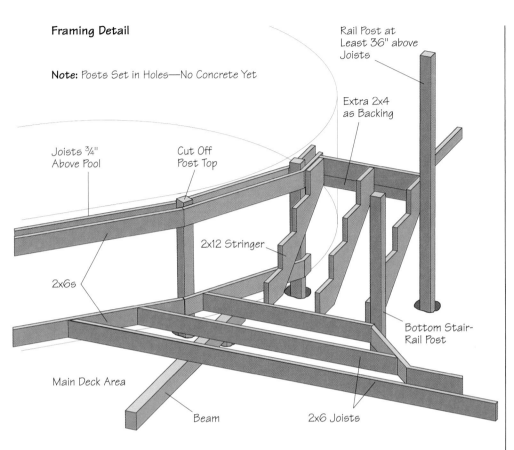

Rail Post at Least 36" above Joists

Extra 2x4 as Backing

Cut Off Post Top

Joists ¾" Above Pool

2x12 Stringer

2x6s

Main Deck Area

Beam

2x6 Joists

Bottom Stair-Rail Post

Providing Access to the Area Beneath

For the skirting, make sure you have top and bottom nailing surfaces that are plumb with each other. Cut lengths of 1x6 to fit so that they come within about 1 inch of the ground. Attach them to the outside joists and bottom nailers.

You'll need to get under the deck from time to time to maintain your pool, and you may want some storage space as well. To build simple but sturdy access panels, sandwich factory-made lattice panels between two 2x4s as shown. Attach them to the joist and nailer with screws. If you think you'll need to remove the panels more than once a month, hang the panels using strap hinges, eyescrews, and hooks.

Access Panel

Framing Detail for additional information.)

Laying the Decking

Around the curved ends of the pool, you can install the decking so that it overhangs the pool, then cut a curved line so the overhang is 1 inch or so. To do this, use the pool itself as a reference for establishing the line. As an alternative, cap the edges of the decking with 2x6 trim, as shown in the rendering and plan view (pages 87 and 88).

To support the narrow section of pool surround trim, use short pieces of 2x6. For the butt joints on the pool surround trim, angle-cut the decking pieces to 15 degrees, laying them as you go. If necessary, adjust the angle on your last cuts to make it come out all right.

Build the benches as described on page 97. For the bench that runs alongside the pool, build a simple frame out of 2x4s, making it 17 inches high.

To provide access to the pool mechanism, Drummond constructed a removable decking section. To maintain a seamless look, install the decking before you cut this opening, keeping track of where you need to locate the "trap door." Using a circular saw and then a handsaw or reciprocating saw, cut the decking flush to the inside edges of the joists below. Screw the cutout pieces to lengths of 2x2 to make a simple panel. Attach nailers to the joists, setting them at a proper height to ensure a smooth decking surface once the panel is in place. Drill a fingerhole or two into the trap door using a 1½-inch spade or Forstener bit.

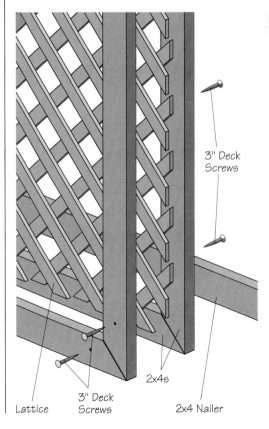

3" Deck Screws

Lattice

3" Deck Screws

2x4s

2x4 Nailer

Getting It All in a Small Space

*T*hough it ranks as one of this book's easiest decks to build, this is no boxy affair that looks as if it were slapped together. With all of its style, you can build it over a weekend or two with the help of an able-bodied friend—and without shelling out a lot for materials.

Ground View

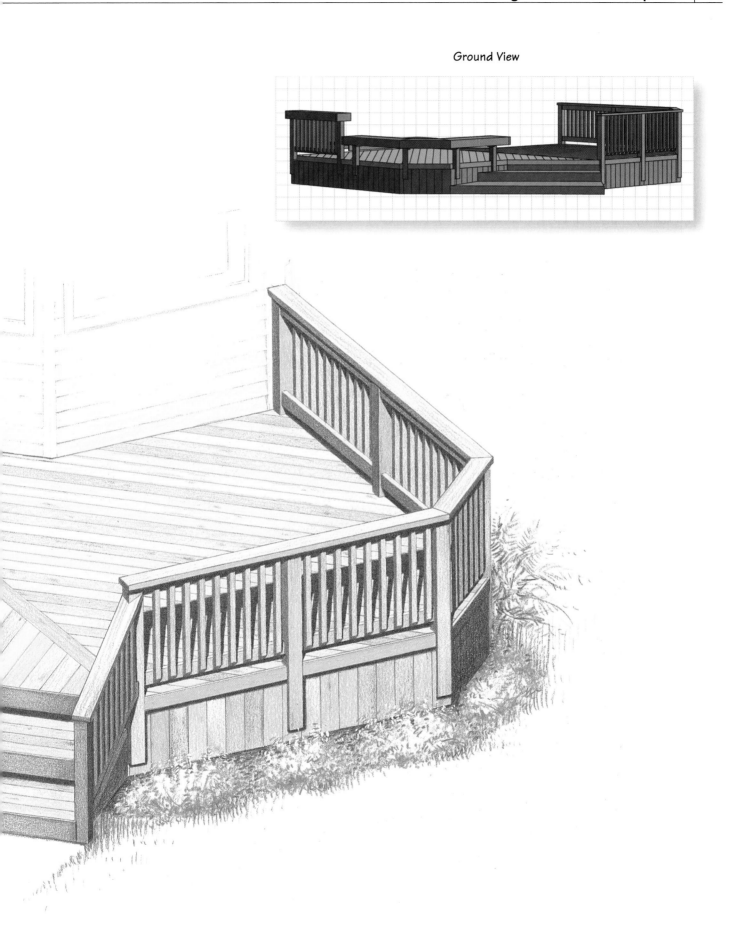

Getting It All in a Small Space, Plan View

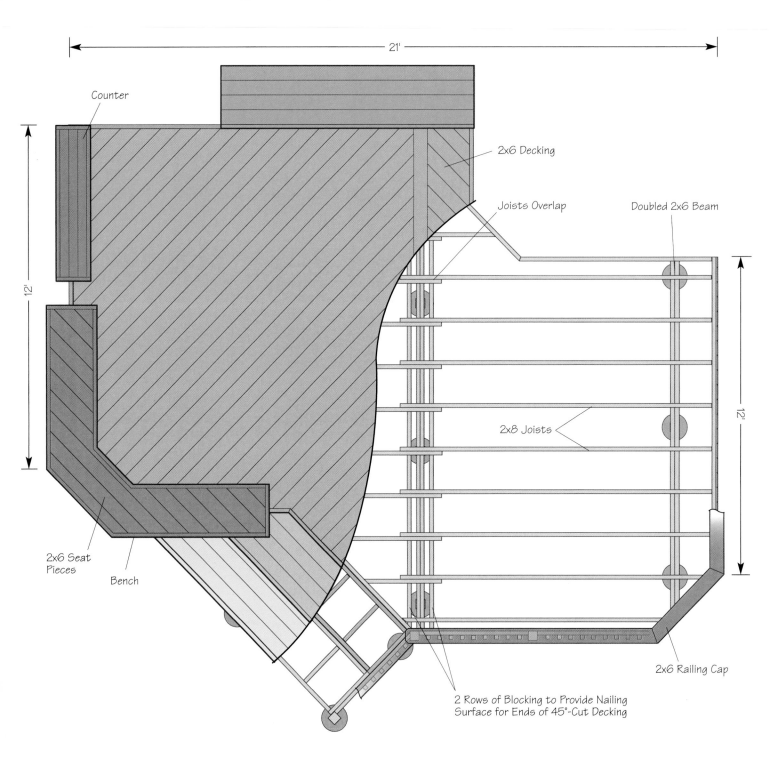

Counter

21'

2x6 Decking

Joists Overlap

Doubled 2x6 Beam

12'

2x8 Joists

12'

2x6 Seat
Pieces

Bench

2x6 Railing Cap

2 Rows of Blocking to Provide Nailing
Surface for Ends of 45°-Cut Decking

Design Considerations

Only where the deck meets the house will you find a 90-degree angle on the deck proper. Though the sides measure the same length, they are offset to foil the symmetry, and one of them has a rail, while the other has a bench. The spacious steps that lead down to the lawn are set at an angle, emphasizing the deck as a transition from house to yard.

Space Efficiency. Drummond figures that this structure is about as small as a deck can get and still contain the work and entertainment areas that most people want. The deck measures only 220 square feet and appears to form a single shape, yet the surface area provides

■ A dining area (to the right of the rear-entry door, looking from the yard)

■ A food-preparation space (on the other side of the door)

■ A set of 18-inch-wide steps that offers room for socializing

■ A direct line of travel to the yard, so traffic can flow unimpeded, even when all three areas are in use.

Orienting this deck properly to the house's rear entry helped to maximize its usefulness. A small landing just outside the door allowed Drummond to lower the main deck 7 inches, which improves the view of the yard from the house and helps define the deck as a separate space, so it doesn't seem like a mere extension of the house.

The angled steps leading down to the yard provide an appealing focal point. An out-of-the-ordinary feature such as this costs little in the way of time and material, but it helps to transform an otherwise plain deck into a more interesting place.

Elevation with Bench

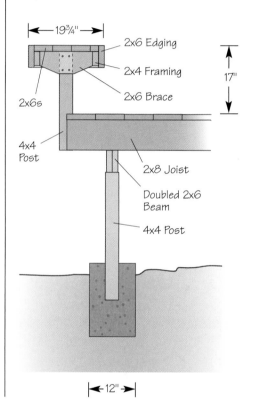

- 19¾"
- 2x6 Edging
- 2x4 Framing
- 17"
- 2x6 Brace
- 2x6s
- 4x4 Post
- 2x8 Joist
- Doubled 2x6 Beam
- 4x4 Post
- 12"

Materials Used for This Deck

Framing	4x4 posts 4x6s or doubled 2x6s for beams 2x8 joists			2x6 seat braces 2x6 seat pieces and edging
Decking	2x6s	Hardware		Joist hangers for 2x8s Angled joist hangers for 2x8s Angle brackets Fasteners for joist hangers 3" deck screws or 10d galvanized nails 3" lag screws with washers for railing and bench posts 2½" deck screws for attaching balusters
Skirt	1x6 verticals 2x4 edging			
Railing	4x4 posts (also used as structural posts) 2x6 railing cap 2x4 top and bottom rails 2x2 balusters			
Benches	4x4 posts 2x4 framing pieces	Masonry		Concrete Concrete tube forms

Construction Techniques

This straightforward design offers few surprises. The footings shown are fine for Virginia and other areas that don't sustain heavy frosts, but check with your building department to see whether the local code requires deeper footings or different post anchors.

Framing With Overlapping Joists

Because the joists span more than 20 feet, you'll need to split them on a beam. The easiest way is to overlap them; that is, let them run past each other on the beam, as shown in the Plan View on page 94. That way, you won't have to cut the joists to exact length. This technique does, however, yield two offset rows of decking screws rather than a single straight line. If that bothers you, cut the joists to length, butt them together, and join them using mending plates. Or you can scab a 2x4 to the side of the offset joist to accept nailing from the decking, thus keeping the nailing straight. Also, you can eliminate surface nailing altogether by using any of the blind fasteners on the market. They are more expensive, however.

Lay out the footings, and then place the posts, leaving them longer than needed. (You'll cut them all to exact height once you've placed them.) Temporarily brace the posts using 2x8s and screws (in a similar way to the detail drawing on page 116). Set a water level, line level, or carpenter's level on a long, straight board to establish a uniform height for the

posts. If you intend to have a single 7-inch-high step and a 1-inch drop at the door, this height should measure 20$\frac{1}{2}$ inches below the level of the interior floor at the threshold. Now, cut the posts.

If you're building doubled 2x8 beams, make them longer than they need to be. Set the beams on top of the posts, and temporarily brace them. (See "Bracing & Supporting the Beams," on page 57, except you won't be working so high in the air.) Construct the framing for the main deck, starting with two of the long (split) joists and the outside joists (headers) into which they butt. Once you've installed the inside joists, cut the beams to length and install the rim joists.

Angled Decking with a Divider Strip

Make sure you include the two rows of blocking pieces, as shown in the Plan View, so that you'll have ample nailing surface for the diagonally cut ends of the decking boards.

Chalk a line down the center of the deck, centering it where the middle decking strip will go. Cut and firmly install the two rows of blocking, positioning each of them 4 inches away from the chalk line.

Unless you're a skilled carpenter, don't attempt to run diagonal decking that meets in a series of V shapes in the middle of the deck. (For an example of this treatment, see

Framing the Steps

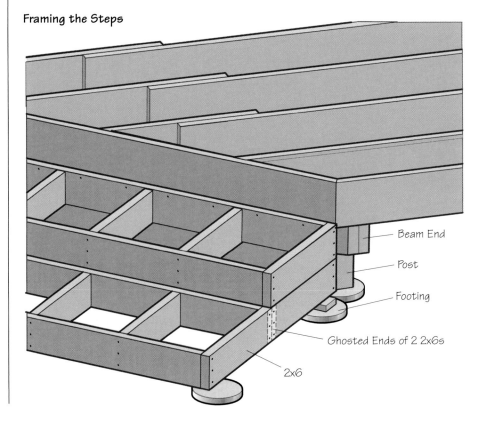

Beam End

Post

Footing

Ghosted Ends of 2 2x6s

2x6

"Stately and Symmetrical," pages 150 and 151.) Because few people can make perfect angles and boards vary slightly in width, you'll have an extremely difficult time getting all the pieces to meet precisely. Instead, it's a better idea to run a 2x6 divider strip down the middle of the deck and then butt the diagonally cut ends of the decking against the divider. This technique allows you to be off by as much as about $^1/_8$ inch or so without its being noticeable.

Use an arrow-straight piece for the divider strip. Stretch a string line to make absolutely sure it's straight, and anchor it firmly so it won't move when you butt the decking against it when nailing down the boards.

Cut a number of decking pieces to 45 degrees on one end. Starting in the middle, lay one piece on either side of the center strip exactly opposite each other. Use a line to make sure the pieces are straight, and lay the remaining decking. Finish the job with chalk-line cuts on the ends, allowing the decking to overhang the outside joists and headers by $1^1/_2$ inches.

Building the Bench

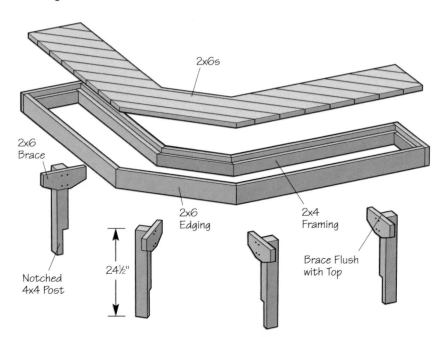

2x6s

2x6 Brace

2x6 Edging

2x4 Framing

Brace Flush with Top

Notched 4x4 Post

24½"

Framing Deep Stairs Leading to the Yard

You'll need to adjust the number and height of these stairs to suit your yard. Make them at least 16 inches deep and no more than 8 inches in rise, so they'll be comfortable to sit on as well as to climb and descend.

Build the frames, and temporarily support them. The steps need to be supported separately from the main deck. For this purpose, use posts or

Divider Strip

concrete tube forms. Once you've finished the framing, pour concrete for all the footings.

Drummond's Bench Design

Drummond uses this bench on many of his decks, and many other builders use similar designs on their structures. **Note:** Do not use this design unless your bench will turn a corner as shown here; otherwise, it will lack lateral strength and will wobble.

Cut the bench posts $24^1/_2$ inches long and make $1^3/_4$x$8^3/_4$-inch notches at the bottom where the posts meet the deck. For each post, cut a 2x6 brace to the dimensions shown in the detail drawing. Firmly attach the braces to the tops of the posts, drilling pilot holes and driving five $2^1/_2$-inch screws for each. Notch the decking, and anchor the posts to the deck at the corners, drilling pilot holes and driving two 3-inch lag screws with washers into each.

Attach the 2x4 framing to the posts, and then check to make sure everything is square. Attach the 2x6 edging to the framing pieces, using a scrap piece of 2x4 to align it $1^1/_2$ inches above the top edges of the framing. Fill in with the 2x6 seat pieces, cutting them carefully to fit snugly. Use the pattern shown to create a distinctive appearance as well as to provide greater strength.

Brace Detail

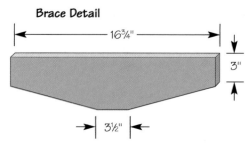

16¾"

3"

3½"

Twin Decks Surrounding a Porch

*T*he homeowners' house had a rectangular screened back porch with a simple set of steps leading down to the yard. Because traffic flowed right through the middle of the porch, there was no good place to dine or lounge. The homeowners do a lot of entertaining, so they wanted more usable space as well as clearly defined areas. Drummond's solution called for rebuilding the porch as well as installing twin decks.

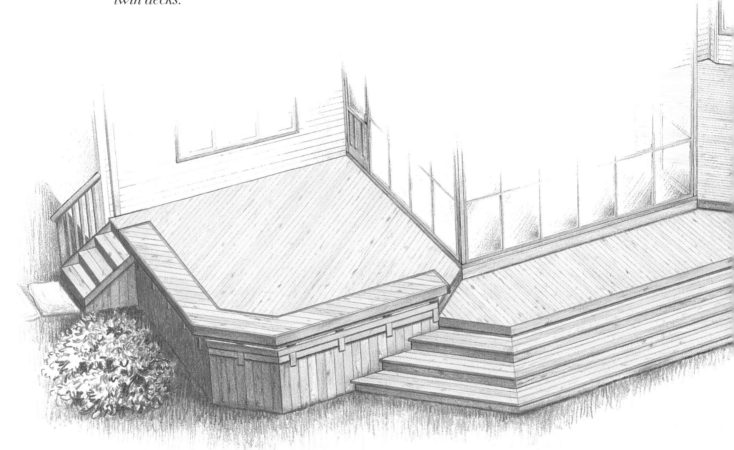

Ground View

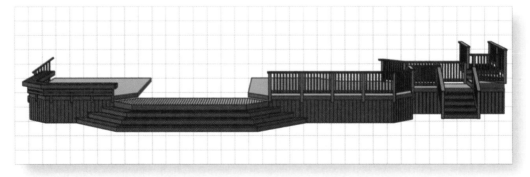

Drummond thus decided to reroute traffic through the porch. He tore out the existing screening and installed two doors, one on each side and close to the house. This freed up most of the porch for dining and lounging.

Deck Wings. Each of the doors leads to a separate deck area: a sun deck with benches to the right and a dining/cooking deck to the left. Although smaller, the sun deck has a more spacious and relaxed feel because it usually contains less furniture. The dining/cooking deck has ample room for a table with chairs as well as a barbecue.

This house has vinyl siding, which can easily be damaged by heat. Drummond cautioned the owners about this, so they located their grill 6 feet away from the house. Keep this in mind if your siding is made of vinyl or other flammable material.

Like many homes in warm climates, this one has heat-pump units (which also provide air conditioning) that are situated outdoors. Homes in other areas may have air-conditioning units located outside. A walkway leads around the outdoor units and into the house via a utility room that is near a bathroom. This allows guests who are on the deck easy access to the bathroom; it also leaves the pump units accessible but not visually exposed.

To the east of the house, a park provides a fine view, and the owners wanted to give guests ample opportunity to gaze in that direction. They also wanted to connect the two decks. Drummond addressed both problems gracefully by adding a small deck to the east of the porch with three spacious stairs that lead down to the lawn. The two larger deck areas remain clearly separate, but the steps allow easy movement between them and provide a perfect place from which to admire the view.

Design Considerations

A screened porch provides welcome refuge during those nights when the mosquitoes are swarming, but it doesn't offer the outdoor feel of a genuine deck. The ideal situation for many people is to have both.

The existing screened porch was one of the "stick-'em-on" types often added by home builders as an afterthought. A simple rectangle, it had little visual appeal. Worse than that, it had a major design flaw: the locations of the entry door and the screened door leading outside created the traffic problem mentioned in the introduction at left, which rendered the porch useless for entertaining.

Twin Decks Surrounding a Porch, Plan View

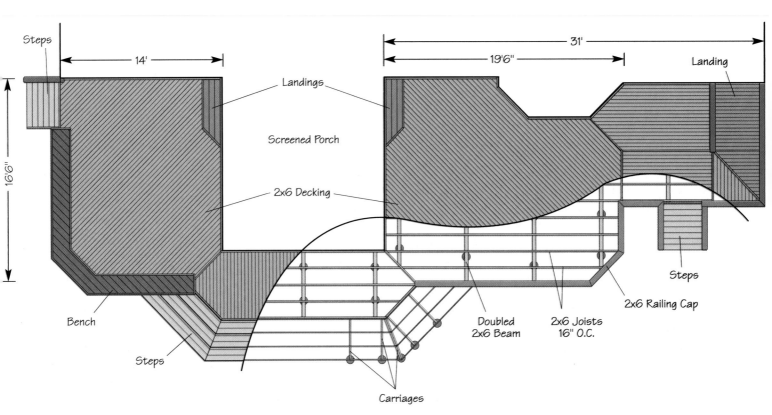

Steps

Landings

Screened Porch

2x6 Decking

Bench

Steps

14'

16'6"

31'

19'6"

Landing

Steps

2x6 Railing Cap

Doubled
2x6 Beam

2x6 Joists
16" O.C.

Carriages

Materials Used for This Deck		
Framing	4x4 posts Doubled 2x8s for beams 2x6 joists 2x12 carriages for stairways	2x6 seat braces 2x6 seat pieces and edging
Decking (approx. 260 sq. ft.)	2x6s 1x4 edging	Hardware Joist hangers for 2x6s Angled joist hangers for 2x6s Angle brackets Fasteners for joist hangers 3" deck screws 3" lag screws with washers for rail and bench posts 2½" deck screws 3½" screws with concrete shields
Skirting	1x6 vertical pieces	
Railing	4x4 posts 2x6 railing cap 2x4 top and bottom rails 2x2 balusters	
Bench	4x4 posts 2x4 framing pieces 2x4 banding pieces	Masonry Concrete Concrete tube forms or lumber for building forms Solid concrete blocks for footings

Construction Techniques

This deck rambles a bit and has several different levels. When laying it out, make sure that the levels will be oriented correctly in relation to each of the doors. Also, take into account the slope of the yard, if any, and carefully determine where the stairway will end. If you miscalculate, you may have to add another step, which could cause the deck to protrude farther into the yard than you want.

Screening in a Porch

Though a screened porch has a relaxed feel, it requires careful planning and construction: mosquitoes have a way of finding even tiny openings. For this reason, it's best to stick with a simple rectangle. More complicated shapes require numerous screened sections. If you'll be screening in a previously open porch, plan the job carefully to minimize the number of small sections you'll have to cover.

In addition, consider whether it makes more sense to install the screens permanently or make them removable. If you go with the latter option, you may find it more practical to purchase screened window units from a specialty shop. If you'd rather build them yourself, consider using metal or plastic stock that is designed for the purpose, rather than building them out of wood.

Framing for Widening Stairs

To provide adequate backing for the stair carriages, attach a 2x8 below the 2x6 outside joist. Cut and install standard carriages every 2 to 3 feet, and support their bottoms with concrete footings or a slab. Make sure that all the standard carriages are square to the 2x8 backing piece. At the 45-degree corners, leave room for a middle carriage.

The tricky part is to support the two sets of side treads at the points where they meet the middle steps at a 45-degree angle (forming a supplementary 135-degree angle). Here, a regular-size carriage would be too short, so it's best to cut the treads to fit after you've installed the standard carriages. Using a power miter saw, make $22^{1}/_{2}$-degree cuts on the ends where they meet (to yield complementary $67^{1}/_{2}$-degree angles). Set them in place, and then measure for a double carriage that will run through the middle of the miter joint. This carriage need not fit precisely, but it should provide support for all the tread pieces.

Stair Detail

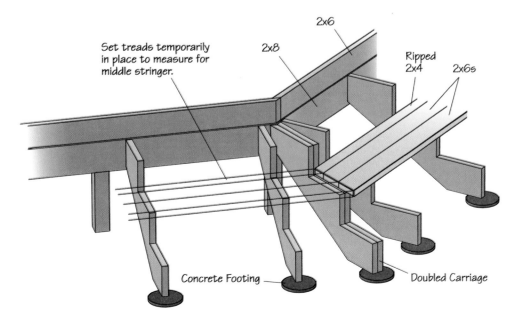

Set treads temporarily in place to measure for middle stringer.

2x6

2x8

Ripped 2x4

2x6s

Concrete Footing

Doubled Carriage

Elevation

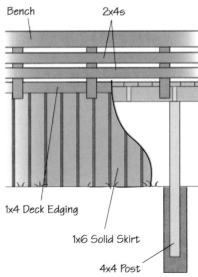

Bench

2x4s

1x4 Deck Edging

1x6 Solid Skirt

4x4 Post

Cozy Deck
with Benches and Planters

The homeowners wanted a deck that would provide a smooth transition from the house to the pool and help to focus attention on the pool. They wanted plenty of planter space for flowers as well. Drummond came up with an unusual bench/planter to take care of these latter two requirements. He positioned it so that people sitting on it would face the pool.

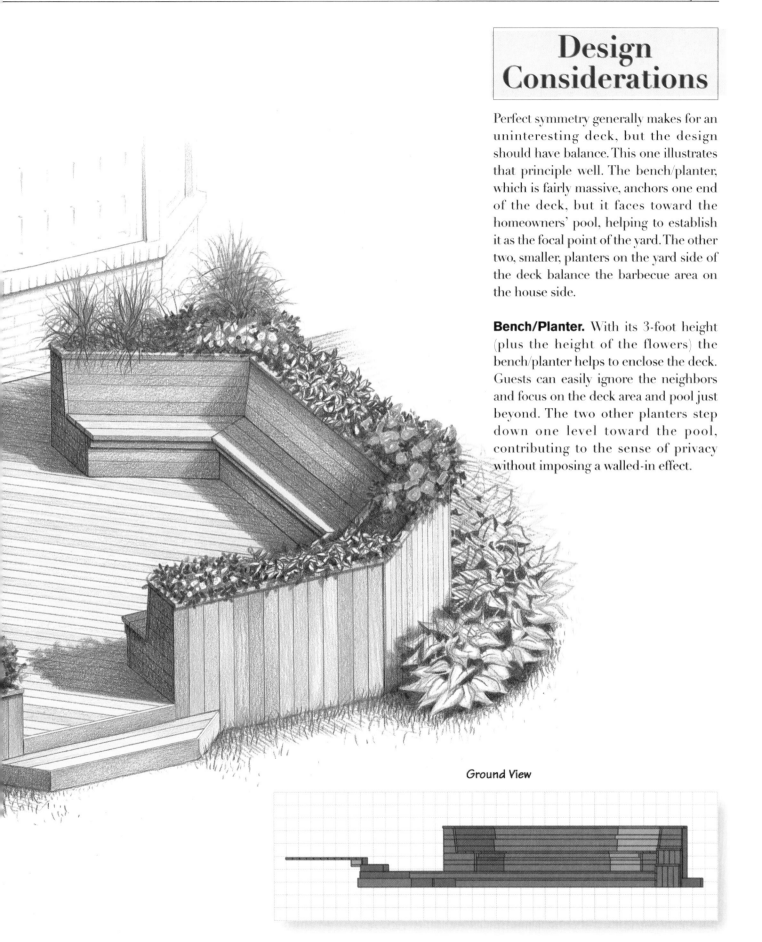

Design Considerations

Perfect symmetry generally makes for an uninteresting deck, but the design should have balance. This one illustrates that principle well. The bench/planter, which is fairly massive, anchors one end of the deck, but it faces toward the homeowners' pool, helping to establish it as the focal point of the yard. The other two, smaller, planters on the yard side of the deck balance the barbecue area on the house side.

Bench/Planter. With its 3-foot height (plus the height of the flowers) the bench/planter helps to enclose the deck. Guests can easily ignore the neighbors and focus on the deck area and pool just beyond. The two other planters step down one level toward the pool, contributing to the sense of privacy without imposing a walled-in effect.

Ground View

Cozy Deck, Plan View

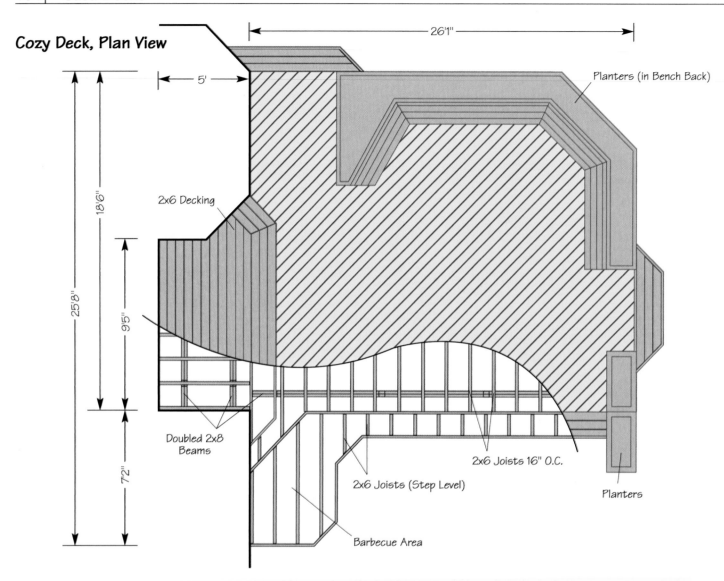

26'1"

5'

18'6"

25'8"

9'5"

7'2"

2x6 Decking

Planters (in Bench Back)

Doubled 2x8
Beams

2x6 Joists (Step Level)

2x6 Joists 16" O.C.

Planters

Barbecue Area

Materials Used for This Deck

Framing	4x4 posts Doubled 2x8s for beams 2x6 joists		Hardware	Joist hangers for 2x6s Angled joist hangers for 2x6s Angle brackets Fasteners for joist hangers 3" deck screws 3" lag screws with washers for bench posts 2½" deck screws 3½" screws with concrete shields
Decking	2x6s 1x6 and 1x8 edging			
Bench/Planter and Planters	4x4 posts 2x4 framing pieces 2x6 & 2x4 banding & seat back pieces 2x6 seat braces 2x6 seat pieces 1x6 tongue-and-groove for the rear skirting 15-lb. roofing felt for lining		Masonry	Concrete Concrete tube forms or lumber for building forms Solid concrete blocks for footings

Design Considerations (cont'd)

The bench/planter does triple duty: It offers comfortable seating, generous planting space, and easily accessible storage beneath the lift-up seat panels. The entire bench sits on top of the decking, which forms the floor of the storage compartments.

The Finer Points. The multiple levels of this deck seem to cascade gently toward the pool. A landing at the entry door provides just enough room for a couple of chairs and a small table. From there, a single step drops down to the main deck. As you approach the pool, another step down to the patio surface is gracefully emphasized by the planters, one of which sits on the main deck, the other on the patio.

Against the house, there's room for a modest-size barbecue. At about 4½ by 6 feet, it falls short of Drummond's recommended 5x8-foot minimum for a cooking area. But because it sits slightly above the patio surface, it works well enough.

At the homeowners' request, Drummond rounded off the edges of all decking boards. This subtle touch emphasizes the joints between the boards, creating a distinctive effect. If the boards cup slightly, which is common, it also lessens the likelihood that water will collect in the small valleys. The same effect can be achieved by using specially milled grooved-and-beveled decking.

Elevation

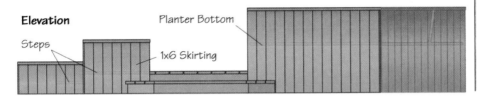

Steps
Planter Bottom
1x6 Skirting

Construction Techniques

If part of the deck rests on an existing patio surface, you may not need to install footings there. However, if the frost line in your area is more than 6 inches deep, it's best to pour footings rather than risk the possibility of frost heave. Most patios measure only 4 to 6 inches deep, which means that they rise and fall slightly as the seasons change. If part of the deck moves and the rest of it doesn't, boards could crack.

The decking is cut flush to the outside joists, and then a 1x6 or 1x8 piece is attached to the face. The top edge of this piece, which serves as both edging and fascia, aligns flush with the deck surface. This approach is riskier than the usual practice of letting the decking overhang the fascia by an inch or so. To play it safe, make sure you use dry lumber (like clear redwood) that won't shrink or warp, and attach it securely; other-

wise, unsightly gaps may open up after a year or so.

Small Ground-Level Sections. If your deck includes a small area off to the side, such as the cooking space on this one, you may find it tempting to skimp on—or even skip—the footings. After all, it seems like a lot of work for such a small area. However, resist the temptation: always support every part of a deck with full footings that extend below the frost line.

In some cases, you may get away with taking the easy way out—for instance, by resting the framing on precast concrete piers that sit in the ground rather than pouring bona fide footings. At worst, the piers probably will rise an inch or less while the rest of the deck stays put. If the small section stands mostly on its own as a peninsula, the rise-and-fall may not damage

your deck. Keep in mind, however, that you'll have to get your local building department's approval for all footings.

Planter/Bench. Build the planter as shown on page 85, except that the inside boards run horizontally, with two 2x4s to add visual interest. In front of the planter sits the bench, basically an extension of the lower part of the planter, with a lid made of 2x6s and 2x4s.

Bench Seat, Raised

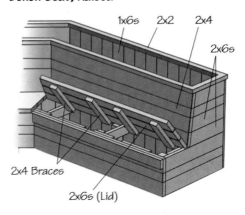

1x6s   2x2   2x4
2x6s
2x4 Braces
2x6s (Lid)

Making a Square Deck Livelier

*Y*ears ago, a previous owner had added a stodgy, rectangular deck onto the homeowners' house. When the homeowners called in Drummond, they had no complaints about the deck's usefulness, and it provided ample room for everything they needed to do. But they still felt that they had outgrown it: Their yard had developed into a thing of beauty, which left the deck looking like a poor relation. The homeowners' purpose in modifying the deck was strictly to spruce up its appearance. Drummond proposed that they cut off two corners and add a large circular section.

Ground View

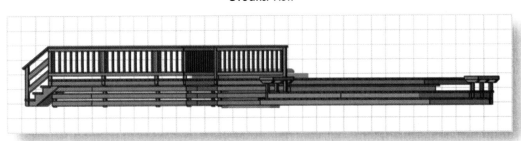

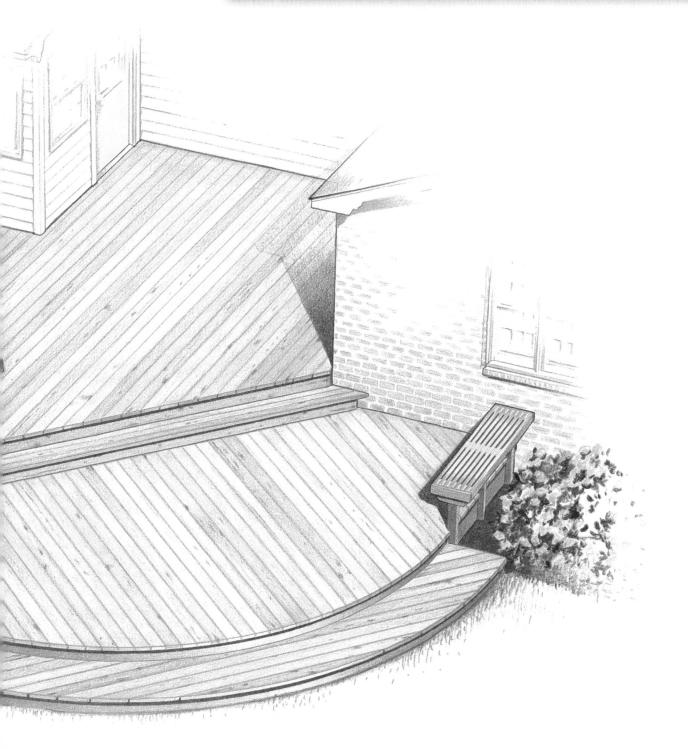

Making a Square Deck Livelier, Plan View

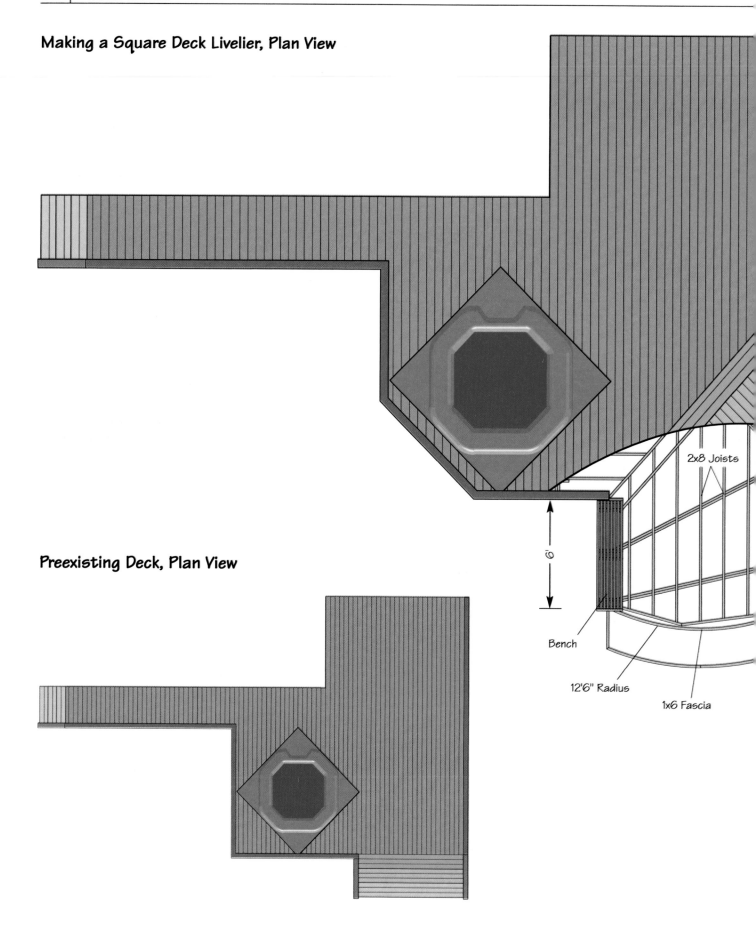

2x8 Joists

6'0"

Preexisting Deck, Plan View

Bench

12'6" Radius

1x6 Fascia

Design Considerations

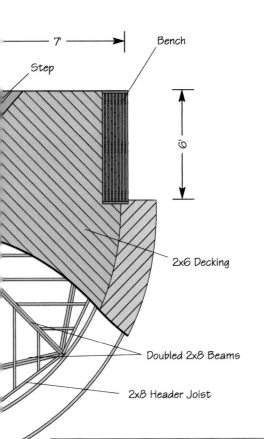

7'

Step

Bench

6'

2x6 Decking

Doubled 2x8 Beams

2x8 Header Joist

This design departs from Drummond's usual precepts about functional areas. He calls it an "impact deck," intended as a visual statement that would make a dull deck exciting. It provides room for a table with chairs, but a great deal of space could be considered wasted because it has no clearly assigned use. Sometimes, however, "wasted" space can lend an air of expansiveness and luxury.

The circular addition provides a graceful transition to the yard. Because this area sprawls expansively, a person walking on it does not feel funneled in a particular direction. The wooden surface fans out and seems more a part of the lawn and landscape than a stairway toward it.

Adding on. If you have a squarish deck that lacks style, resist the temptation to tear it down and start over from scratch. You can probably save some money as well as labor by adding on to the structure instead. A solution that works for a lot of homeowners is to cut out a triangular area and attach a new section of decking that runs at an angle to the existing deck. If you then add a distinctive curve or some unusual angles and put in a bench or a new style of railing, you'll hardly remember the ho-hum structure that stood there before.

Chances are that you won't be able to match the existing decking exactly. The old surface will have weathered or may have been built from material that is now hard to find at the local lumberyard or mill. However, most of Drummond's add-on clients find that a difference in color or texture is not displeasing to the eye, especially if the new surface begins one step up or down, as with this deck. For extremely different wood colors, a deck stain—either semitransparent or solid-color depending on the severity of the problem—will hide any discrepancy.

Materials Used for This Deck

Framing	4x4 posts		Angle brackets
	Doubled 2x8s for beams		Fasteners for joist hangers
	2x8 joists		3" deck screws
	2x6 joists for step		3" lag screws with washers for bench posts
Decking	2x6s		2½" deck screws
			3½" screws with concrete shields
Benches	2x4s for seat pieces		
	1x4 spacers between seat pieces	Masonry	Concrete
	2x4 braces		Concrete tube forms or lumber for building forms
	4x4 posts		Solid concrete blocks for footings
Hardware	Joist hangers for 2x6s & 2x8s		
	Angled joist hangers for 2x6s & 2x8s		

Construction Techniques

This deck is less complicated than it appears, but you'll need to work carefully and pay attention to details. Before you begin cutting, make sure the old deck has adequate support. Also, avoid shortcuts when marking and cutting the curve.

Cutting an Old Deck to Prepare for an Addition

Preparing for the addition will probably take less time than you imagine. Using a circular saw and a reciprocating saw, you can cut away the old decking in a couple of hours. But again, support the deck properly before you start, and plan your cuts carefully to avoid any unpleasant surprises.

Temporary Support. If possible, remove fascia pieces and header joists so that you can climb under the existing deck and assess the situation. If there isn't enough clearance for this, then cut the decking to create access from above. Wherever there's a post or footing that you'll bypass with your cut, check to see that the existing joists will be well supported after you've made your cuts.

The temporary supports needn't be anything elaborate. Lay a short scrap of 2x6 on the ground, and then cut another piece of 2x6 long enough that it will wedge in tightly beneath the joist or joists. Attach the two pieces using toenails or angled screws to keep them from sliding out of position. If you have a number of joists to support, use a 4x4 as a header as shown (opposite).

Removing the Existing Structure. Chalk a line, and then cut away the decking. Next, use a circular saw and a reciprocating saw to cut the joists from underneath. You may have to cut them back by as much as 3³/4 inches: 1¹/2 inches to accommodate a new header joist, ³/4 inch for the fascia piece, and 1¹/2 inches to allow for decking overhang.

Building a Large Curved Section

Install the beams so that they meet in the center of the curve, as shown in the Plan View on page 108. Install the double center joist first, and then run the angled joists wild. (You'll cut them to size after you've installed them all.) Tack a nail at the reference point, and then attach a string and pencil to it. Mark the radius on top of the joists to indicate where you want the framing to end—probably 2¹/4 inches short of the decking to allow for a ³/4-inch fascia and a 1¹/2-inch overhang. Hold straight boards in

Elevation

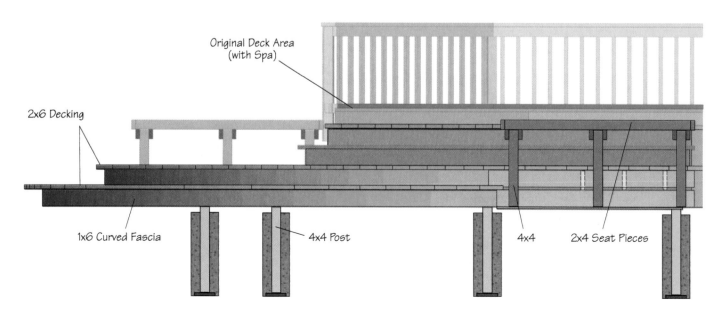

Original Deck Area
(with Spa)

2x6 Decking

1x6 Curved Fascia   4x4 Post   4x4   2x4 Seat Pieces

position to establish the header joist locations, and then mark each joist for cutting. Cut the joists using a circular saw, and install the header joists.

For the fascia board, Drummond finds that a regular 1x6 or 1x8 is flexible enough to bend into position. Hold it (or them) in position, and mark for cutting. Install the decking, allowing it to run wild so that each piece overhangs the fascia by at least $1^1/2$ inches.

To cut the decking, Drummond uses a router equipped with a straight bit. It takes four passes to cut through $1^1/2$-inch-thick lumber. He makes a simple trammel beam from a length of 1x4, drilling a hole for the router bit and then mounting the router on it. He attaches the board to the radius point using a nail driven through a drilled hole so that it will swing freely. **Note:** This will require using a heavy-duty router equipped with a long, straight bit with a $1/2$-inch shank.

Slotted Benches

Because the benches do not have angles, they need to be anchored securely. One is attached to the house with masonry screws, and the other is screwed into the old deck. If possible, use posts that run up from the footings for extra strength. Otherwise, anchor them securely to the deck.

Cut the long seat pieces and the spacers. Join them together using 3-inch screws, and check the assembly for squareness as you work. Next, add the end pieces. Cut the posts, attach two braces to the top of each, and check these to be sure they're square. Attach the posts to the deck and the seat to the posts and braces.

Temporary Joist Support

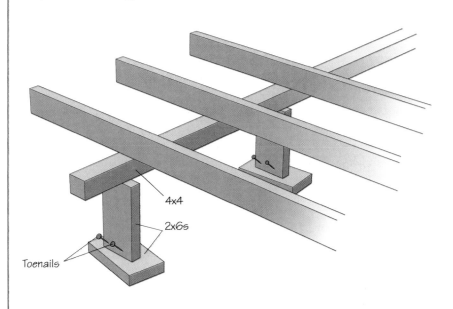

4x4

2x6s

Toenails

Slotted Benches

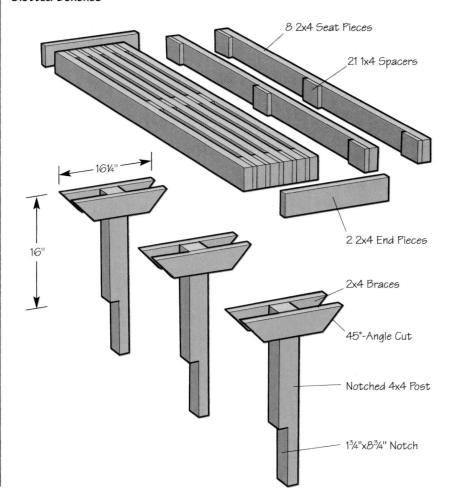

8 2x4 Seat Pieces

21 1x4 Spacers

16¼"

16"

2 2x4 End Pieces

2x4 Braces

45°-Angle Cut

Notched 4x4 Post

1¾"x8¾" Notch

Nearly Square

M *any well-designed decks are longer on one side than another. Such a design approach often improves the appearance of the deck and allows space for several use areas. This deck is nearly square but avoids looking boxy not only because of its angles but also because it contrasts a rail on one side with a bench on the other.*

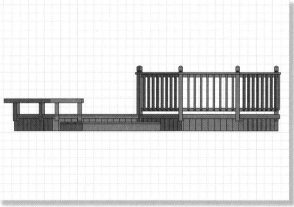

Ground View

Nearly Square, Plan View

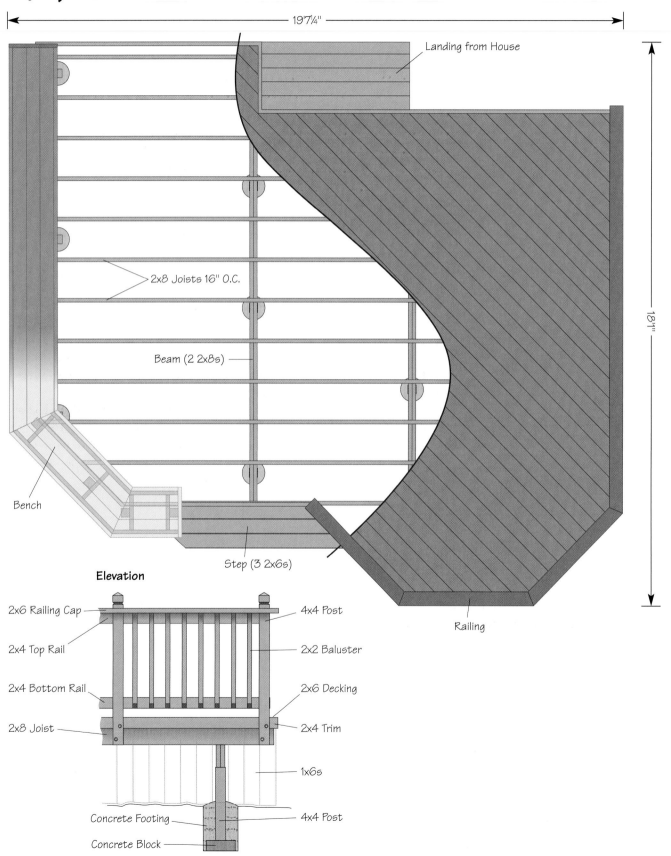

19'7¼"

18'1"

Landing from House

2x8 Joists 16" O.C.

Beam (2 2x8s)

Bench

Step (3 2x6s)

Railing

Elevation

2x6 Railing Cap

2x4 Top Rail

2x4 Bottom Rail

2x8 Joist

4x4 Post

2x2 Baluster

2x6 Decking

2x4 Trim

1x6s

Concrete Footing

Concrete Block

4x4 Post

Design Considerations

The house is built on a concrete slab on grade, which means that the interior floor is only 4 or 5 inches above the ground. Slab houses can pose a problem for deck builders because ideally you should step down onto a deck. In fact, it is often best to lower a deck a full step or two so that the railings will not hinder the view of the yard from inside. (See "Lower Your Deck for a Better View," page 27.)

In this case, the problem was compounded: the yard tended to puddle, and the homeowners wanted to use the deck to solve the moisture problem. However, Drummond advised them that they could not solve the problem of a soggy yard simply by putting a deck on top of it: water would seep through the gaps between the decking, and the shade provided by the deck would make it harder for the ground beneath to dry

out. Depending on how the decking was installed, a good deal of water would run off to one end of the deck. The result would be simply moving the moisture problem from one place to another. So it was important to solve the problem before building the deck. In this case—as in most—it meant changing the grade.

Low Landing. The deck has an unusual feature that you should use only in unusual circumstances. The entry door's threshold is nearly at grade level, and the homeowners wanted the deck raised up a little. So just outside the door is a 2x4-foot landing; the main deck area is one step up from the landing. This design has a disadvantage: Leaves and dirt collect in the small landing. The homeowners were willing to put up with the extra cleaning in order to have a raised deck, however.

The landing's framing consists of 2x2 sleepers that rest on a concrete entry pad. If you live in an area subject to severe frost, you probably couldn't get away with this—you'd need a footing extending below the frost line.

The homeowners originally wanted a deck on two different levels, but this was not possible given that the total area of the deck was to be only about 260 square feet. Splitting such a small deck up would have produced two virtually unusable, tiny deck surfaces. Drummond showed them that by orienting the decking diagonally, he could break up the space visually while maintaining a single surface.

Though small, this deck has all the elements Drummond is after: comfortable eating, food preparation, and conversation areas, as well as a bit of flair.

Materials Used for This Deck

Framing	4x4 posts Doubled 2x8s for beams 2x8 joists for main deck 2x6 framing for step to yard 2x2 sleepers for landing by door		2x6 seat braces 2x6 seat pieces and edging
		Hardware	Joist hangers for 2x8s Angled joist hangers for 2x8s Angle brackets Fasteners for joist hangers 3" deck screws 3" lag screws & washers for railing & bench posts 2½" deck screws 3½" screws with concrete shields
Decking (± 260 sq. ft.)	2x6s 2x4 edging		
Skirting	1x6 vertical pieces 2x4 edging		
Railing	4x4 posts 2x6s for railing cap 2x4 top and bottom rails 2x2 balusters		

		Masonry	Concrete
			Concrete tube forms or lumber for
			   building forms
			Solid concrete blocks for bottoms of
			   footings

Bench	4x4 posts 2x4 framing pieces		

Construction Techniques

The footings described here work for Virginia Beach, where there is little frost. For areas with colder winters, use deeper footings. Resting posts on solid concrete blocks allows Drummond to work on the framing before he pours the concrete—an important time-saver for a professional deck builder. You may want to pour the concrete first, and start framing the next day.

Standard Footings, Posts, and Beams

The deck as shown on page 112 uses 14 footings, three for each of the two outside beams (spaced equally along its length) and four for each of the two inside beams. Lay out the footings on approximate 6-foot centers in each direction, and dig the holes. At the bottom of each hole, tamp the soil firmly with a long 4x4, and set in a solid concrete footing pad. Roughly figure how high the 4x4 posts need to extend upward, and cut them longer than they need to be. You'll cut them to exact size later. Cut the 4x4s square so that they will stand straight on their own. Brace the posts as shown in the drawing at right.

Cut one of the posts near the house to the desired height, and use it as a frame of reference for measuring the other posts. Using a line level, a water level, or a carpenter's level set on top of a long, straight board, mark the other posts, and cut them all.

Construct the beams by gang-nailing 2x8s together, but do not cut them to length yet. Set the beams on the posts, and brace them as shown below. With a low deck such as this, the simple temporary bracing shown will be sufficient.

Framing

Mark the faces of the two small joists, taking into account how they are offset from each other. Cut two of the long joists to exact length, and set them in place, one as far away from the house as possible and the other as close as possible; you may need to temporarily brace them at the beams. Attach the header joists to them.

Now you can fill in the joists between, and then construct the rest of the framing. Once the joists are assembled, cut the beams to size, making their edges flush with the faces of the outside joists. When working with the outside joists next to the house, use scraps of two-by lumber to keep them a uniform distance from the house and to provide stability.

Attach the 2x2 sleepers to the concrete pad near the house, drilling holes with a masonry bit, inserting shields, and driving the screws. Drill countersink holes for the screwheads so that they will not stick up.

Decking with Flush-to-the-Surface Fascia

Drummond cut the 2x6 pressure-treated decking on this deck flush to the face of the outside joists and then edged it with 2x4s rather than let the deck boards overhang an inch or two. This gives the deck a more finished look. Be sure you have good-quality decking wood that will not shrink and is not prone to cracks near the ends of boards. Also, take care that all of the

Temporary Bracing of Posts and Beams

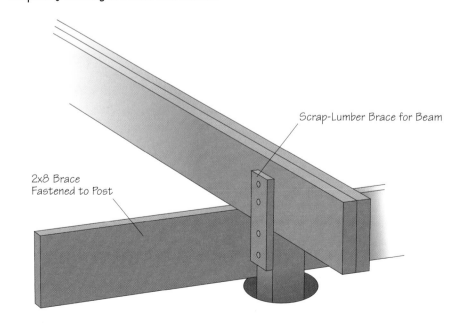

Scrap-Lumber Brace for Beam

2x8 Brace Fastened to Post

outside joists are straight and that the 2x4 trim is relatively knot-free. Otherwise, this detail will make your deck look sloppy rather than finished.

The decking runs at a 45-degree angle to the house. Begin by installing a long, straight piece near the center of the deck, and use it as a frame of reference for the rest of the decking. Many pieces need a 45-degree cut at the end that butts up to the house, so gang-cut them with a power miter saw or a circular saw equipped with a guide.

To maintain a uniform decking line next to the house, tack a temporary one-by spacer on the house, and butt the decking to it.

Once the decking is laid, use a chalk line and circular saw to make cuts so that the decking is flush with the outside joists. Take care to make this cut accurately.

For information on making and installing the bench, see the illustration labeled "Building the Bench," page 97.

Railings with Decorative Post Tops

The top of the railing posts are cut to a point and given a dado band. This feature gives the deck a handcrafted look, and it only takes an hour or two to accomplish.

To make the posts, cut seven 4x4s to about 52 inches, planning your cuts to eliminate as many cracks as possible. On the bottom end of each, cut out a notch 1³/4 inches deep and 8³/4 inches long. Draw a square line around the post, 48 inches from the bottom. From this mark, cut the point at the top of the post with a power

miter saw set at 45 degrees or with a circular saw. Make the first cut as shown; then rotate and cut the post three more times. Using a circular saw set for a 45-degree bevel cut that is ³/4 inch deep, next make a notch cut that goes around the post, about 3 inches below the top mark. (See the detail drawing below.)

Anchor the posts to the deck, making sure they're plumb as you drill pilot holes and drive lag screws. Cut the top and bottom rails to fit between the posts, and fasten them with angle-driven screws.

Next, cut the railing cap pieces: first hold them in position against the inside of the posts to mark them for length. Try to break them on a post or a corner. Then mark and notch them to fit around the posts. The inside edge of the railing cap should be flush with the inside edge of the posts. Fasten the cap pieces with screws.

Install the balusters 6 inches on center, to end up with a railing that has 4¹/2-inch spaces. Drive four screws per 2x2, two on a diagonal at the top and two at the bottom, to make sure the balusters stay firm for years.

Edging and Skirt for a Low Deck

The first step in finishing off this deck is to cut and install the small outside platform step. It's basically a box made of pressure-treated 2x6s that rests on the ground and is nailed to the rim joist of the deck. Make a 45-degree parallelogram from 2x6s. The long sides are 5 feet 10¹/4 inches long. Construct it wide enough to accommodate three 2x6s. Span the area between the outside corner bench post and the last railing post with a couple of 2x8s before attaching the platform.

Next, you'll want to trim the decking. Cut and install the 2x4 edging pieces that cover the cut ends of the decking and fit between the railing posts and the bench posts.

The finishing touch is the skirt. On a deck like this that is only a couple of feet above grade, there is no need for a bottom framing piece to which you would normally anchor the skirt. Cut 1x6 pieces so that, when they are placed vertically, they just reach the level of the grass but do not actually stick into the ground. Attach the 1x6s to the face of the outside joists, butting the bottom of the 2x4 edging.

Cutting the Dado Band

Cutting the Point

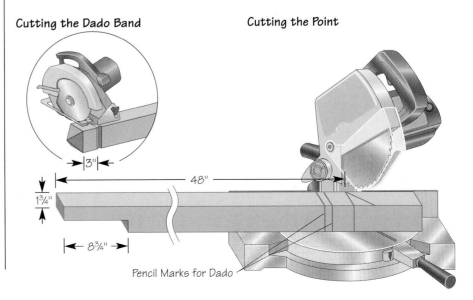

3"

48"

1³/4"

8³/4"

Pencil Marks for Dado

Gary Marsh
All Decked Out®
Novato, California
(415) 897-7623
www.garymarshdesign.com

When not visiting with clients or designing and building decks, Gary Marsh, owner of All Decked Out in Novato, California, spends a good part of his time sculpting in a variety of media. Auto-body putty and clay are two of his favorites. He keeps his workshop surprisingly tidy and organized, despite a profusion of objects that tell of his interests: four or five sculptures in various stages of completion, a professional drafting table, and a serious collection of woodworking tools.

Design Considerations

Marsh brings along his artist's sensibilities when he designs decks for residents of well-to-do Marin County, California. (He also designs for clients all across the United States.) Most of the decks he builds overhang steep slopes that offer sweeping views of San Francisco Bay area. People in these parts typically want a design that reflects their individual tastes; rarely will one of Marsh's clients ask for a deck that looks just like one they see in his presentation book.

Although he designs decks for a living, Marsh believes that they have ruined the appearance of many homes in the United States. While visiting a client on the East Coast, he saw majestic eighteenth-century homes, covered with clapboard and exuding history, that had been compromised by boxy, unimaginative appendages made of unstained pressure-treated lumber. This is an extreme example, but the lesson to be learned applies to all homes: build a deck that will enhance your home—not just a platform on which to barbecue. Marsh takes his own advice to heart, taking extreme care to instill each design with artistry and flair.

▼ *This handsome redwood deck, shown left and below, provides an inviting, relaxing retreat while exhibiting some of Marsh's hallmarks, such as a well-thought-out floor plan, free-flowing design, and exquisite craftsmanship.*

Overcoming Problems

In northern California, Marsh has to deal with some serious engineering and construction challenges. Though the drawings and pictures may not show it, most of his decks overhang hills that could almost be called cliffs. On nearly every project, he has to consult with soil and structural engineers. To ensure that the deck won't slide down the hillside or pull away from the house, he typically digs large-diameter footing holes down to bedrock—and drills 5 to 6 feet into it. Marsh then excavates large trenches for grade beams to join the footings to the house foundation. He reinforces all holes and trenches with steel before pouring massive amounts of concrete. In some cases, he has to hire a large crane to lift structural elements over the house and into place on the down side of the hill.

Such work is not for the do-it-yourselfer. If you have a severe slope, it

would be advisable to call in a professional at least to supply the footings and perhaps to build the entire deck. Your local building department will probably call for a soil test as well as an engineer-approved plan for the structure.

Code Limitations. Besides the challenges of building the understructure, Marsh often encounters code limitations that people in other parts of the country don't have to worry

◀ *Surrounding a 12-foot-high rooftop slate patio, this elegant deck extends the home's living space out into a hillside, a common problem-solving feature of Marsh's decks.*

◀ **Marsh often encounters and must overcome code restrictions** when he builds a deck. Two examples of decks that required ingenuity are the tree-top beauty (far left) and the docklike resting spot on a waterway in California (left).

▼ Detail work such as the edging treatment on the railing cap, visible at left in this photo of a second-level deck with a commanding view, is a signature of Marsh's work.

about. Each town in his area has stringent rules regarding how much square footage is allowed; setback requirements often restrict how far out from the house he can build; and severe-slope regulations set strict limits on how much of the property can be occupied by anything other than erosion-limiting plants. In short, Marsh often finds his creativity shackled by a number of restrictions. His customers attest, however, that he succeeds dramatically.

Techniques to Use

As long as you're not building on a steep incline, you won't have to take the sometimes extreme steps that Marsh does to support his decks. Use standard footings and posts, as described in *Decks: Plan, Design, Build.* (See page 7.) The upper portions of most of Marsh's designs contain a number of stylish features and finishing touches that you can incorporate into your deck if you work with care.

▶ Marsh approaches each job with an open mind. Rather than limit himself to conventional formulas, he spends some time dreaming about the possibilities. As you plan your deck, you'll naturally think in terms of mimicking those you see in your area. But compared with house building, it's usually (but not always—especially in Marsh's unique situations) fairly easy and inexpensive to build a deck that incorporates unusual twists and turns. Don't be afraid to use your imagination.

▶ Because of the tremendous views that many of his clients enjoy, Marsh thinks hard about which way people will face. Whenever possible, he orients a bench so that a person sitting on it won't have to twist around to take in the scenery. This sometimes requires altering the shape of the deck so that occupants won't be forced to stare at the house. The bench shown in "Square Corner with a Twist," pages 146–149, for instance, makes it easy for sitters to choose the view or to gather in a group.

▶ Though Marsh speaks jokingly of being "at one with the wood," he takes lumber selection very seriously. He spends plenty of time both choosing material at the lumberyard and deciding at the job site which pieces will go where. For every part that will be touched when the deck is finished, such as handrails, he reserves the best-quality stock. For pieces that need to remain stable—railing caps, for instance—he uses only certified kiln-dried material. Pieces that will be bent into curves, on the other hand, call for green lumber with a vertical grain. If you're unsure about selecting the right lumber for a particular application, ask for help at the lumberyard.

▶ Although you probably won't need to resort to Marsh's more serious engineering efforts, note how he reinforces some portions of his decks for specific purposes. For example, he avoids the conventional approach of screwing or bolting rail posts to the side of the deck. These will fail over time, especially in situations where extra strength is needed. In almost every deck that Marsh designs and builds, he uses posts that are bolted within the framing for a strong connection. (For a detail on an alternative way to *reinforce* rail posts, see "Sheltered but Open," page 135.)

▶ Marsh uses a variation of an unusual technique for making caps on a curved railing. He cuts the curves out of a piece of 2x12 (or two 1x12s) but doesn't throw away the waste. Instead, he uses the offcuts from one section as parts for others. This requires serious laminating: You must use glue that will stand up to the weather and join the pieces tightly to avoid ending up with a sloppy-looking cap. This will save you a good deal of expensive material.

▶ To enhance the appearance of moldings, Marsh often finishes them using a router equipped with a roundover or chamfer bit. He'll often stop the roundover or chamfer short of the edge of the board to add a distinctive look. (See "Soaking and Dining Areas with Shingles and Siding," page 145, and "Square Corner with a Twist," page 149.)

▶ To bend curved horizontal rail members and fascia pieces, Marsh uses another unconventional technique. Because some boards, for one reason or another, bend more readily than others and some curves are tighter than others, he treats each piece individually. He starts with a green piece of one-by lumber and planes it down until it bends enough for the curve in question. This means that some pieces will be a bit thicker than others, but because several pieces will be joined to make laminated rail or fascia members, the total thicknesses of the members end up identical.

▶ Marsh's planter design is more elaborate than most. It calls for a galvanized metal liner with a downspout. He orders the liners from a sheet-metal shop and builds simple boxes around them. He then positions them carefully so that no structural members will be regularly soaked by the runoff from rainfall or overwatering.

▼ *Overhead structures like this sunscreen* *are common where temperatures get warm and the sun is strong.*

Sweeping Elegance in a Small Space

A stunning pool with waterfall was located only 10 feet from the house. But in this setting, the beauty of the surroundings called for a deck that conveyed a sense of spaciousness. By using curved lines throughout and incorporating a stairway that appears much grander than its actual size, Marsh created a sense of open-ended luxury in a limited space.

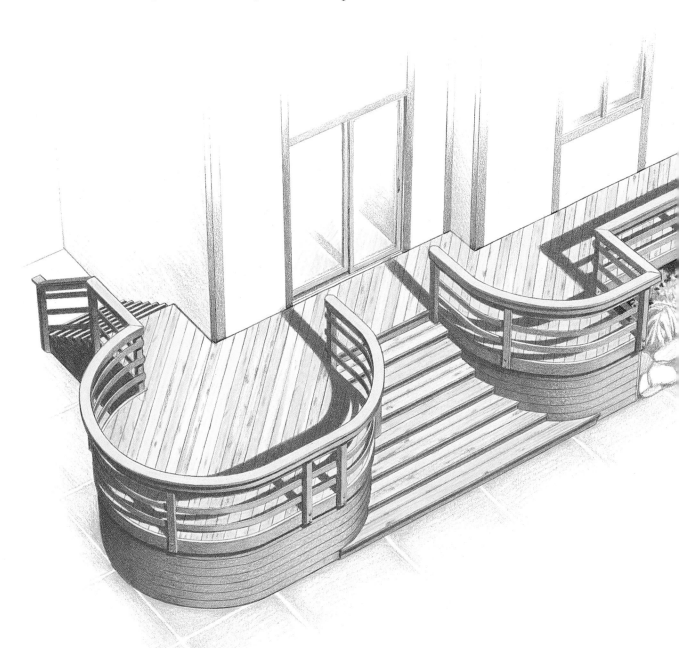

Ground View

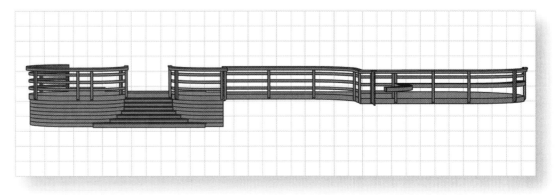

Sweeping Elegance in a Small Space, Plan View

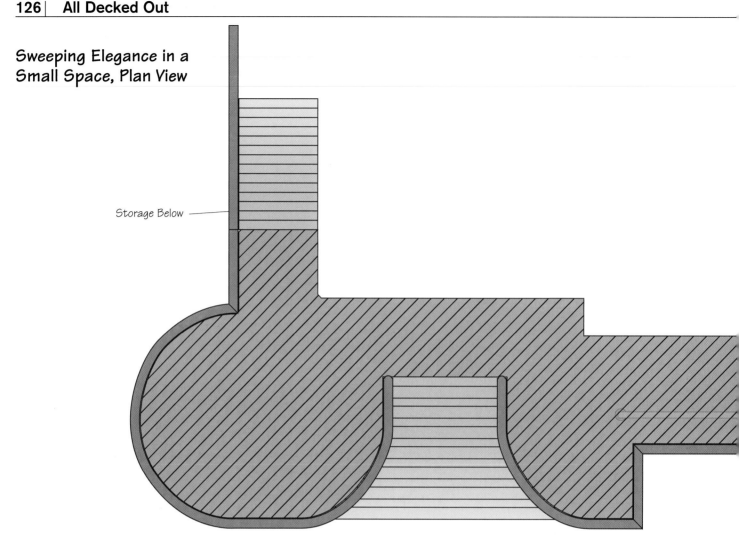

Storage Below ——

Materials Used for This Deck

Framing (pressure-treated pine)	4x8 and 4x6s for beams 2x8 joists 2x8 ledgers and headers 2x12 stair stringers		1x6s, planed and laminated, for curved edging 2x6 seat pieces
Decking	2x6s	Hardware	3½" deck screws Joist hanger nails Post anchors for anchoring posts to concrete T-straps for tying beams to posts Joist hangers for 2x8s Angled joist hangers for 2x8s Angle brackets Lag screws with washers for anchoring the ledger Machine bolts for railing posts
Fascia	1x8s, planed and laminated, for fascia and skirting 1x6s, planed and laminated, for banded skirting		
Railings and bench backs	4x4 posts 2x12 and 2x6 pieces for railing caps 1x4s, planed and laminated, for curved horizontal rails		
Benches	4x4 posts 2x4 framing pieces	Masonry	Concrete Precast concrete piers

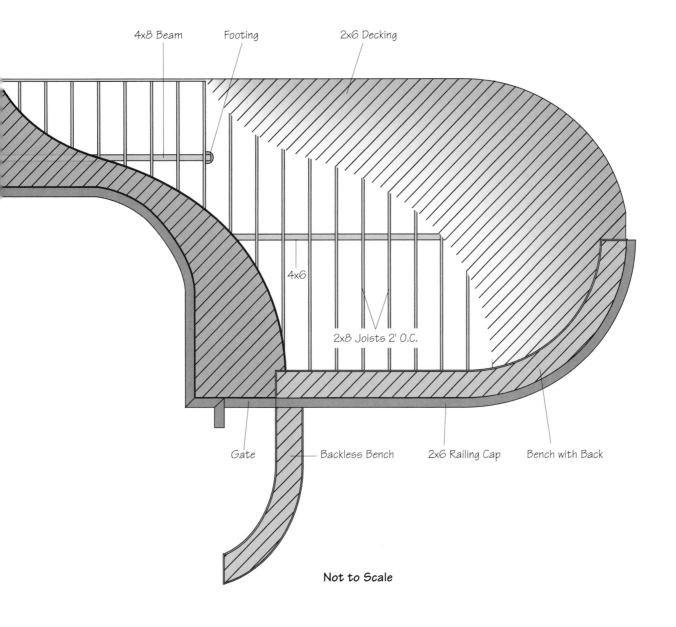

4x8 Beam   Footing   2x6 Decking

4x6

2x8 Joists 2' O.C.

Gate   Backless Bench   2x6 Railing Cap   Bench with Back

Not to Scale

Design Considerations

The homeowners wanted a convenient means of descending to the pool (outside the sliding doors of the house) that wouldn't obstruct the expanse of the deck. In addition, they requested separate areas for sunning and dining.

Marsh met both challenges by incorporating an unusually shaped stairway near one end. It helps to define the circular sunning area next to it without taking up much space. Yet despite the stairway's small footprint, its sides curve away from each other, creating a sense of grandeur. You hardly notice that its steps have only 7½-inch risers and 11-inch treads—dimensions that are usually found only on standard porch or interior stairways.

Aside from the point where the deck meets the house, there's hardly a straight line to be found. The deck jogs and snakes around, partly to follow the contours of the pool, spa, and gardening areas below and partly for aesthetic reasons. Looking out onto a steep backyard filled with a wild profusion of foliage, an angular deck would seem out of place. This one blends nicely with the yard's natural curves and slopes.

Functionality with Style

The deck was planned to be functional as well as aesthetically pleasing. The curved walls that enhance the stairway also hide pool equipment. The center walkway measures only 5 feet wide to accommodate the plantings below. This leaves enough room for guests to lean on the railing and gaze out while traffic flows through comfortably behind them. Between the walkway and the stairway is a barbecue area just large enough for a small charcoal grill and a food-preparation cart. (You could also build a wide shelf into the straight section of railing in this part of the deck as a permanent food-preparation area.)

The main deck provides ample room for dining. A bench with a back follows the circular contours of its perimeter partway around, giving those who sit facing the house a sense of enclosure. For those who'd rather look outward over the lawn, a backless bench extends out into the decorative rockwork area that surrounds the spa.

The elegant railing features a curved cap and three horizontal rails. (The local building codes may not permit such a railing. Check with the building department in your area.) Marsh routed a detail into the caps that gives them a furniture-like appearance.

For the skirting that covers the rounded sections on each side of the steps, he used horizontal bands that mimic the railings above. From ground level, this gives the whole ensemble—steps, skirt, and railing—the appearance of a unified structure rather than that of a basic deck with a few features tacked on.

Front Elevation: Stairs and Railings

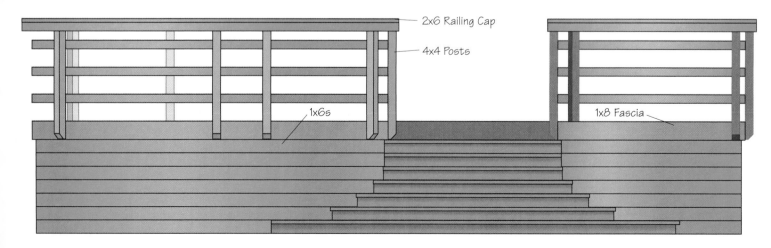

2x6 Railing Cap

4x4 Posts

1x6s

1x8 Fascia

Construction Techniques

Marsh attaches a 2x8 ledger to the house. He supports the 4x8 and 4x6 beams with 4x4 posts that rest on concrete piers set in a bed of poured concrete. Because this is earthquake territory, he uses plenty of T-straps to anchor the beams to the posts.

Installing Curved Horizontal Fascia and Skirting Pieces.

Marsh doesn't soak redwood pieces in water to make them more flexible. He's found that soaked boards often check or twist. (Checking develops when the surface dries faster than the core, causing the grain to separate.)

At the lumberyard, Marsh looks for one-by boards that bend more easily than others. These contain more moisture, but as they dry out they'll grow stiff. To prevent premature drying, keep them out of the sun and covered until you use them. Even an hour in the sun can dramatically change a one-by board's moisture content.

Planing Boards to Bendable Thickness.

Rent or buy a large power planer or jointer that will quickly shave down the boards. With a soft material like redwood or cedar, the work will go quickly provided the jointer's blades are sharp. Plane each piece individually until you think it will bend sufficiently. Then, try carefully bending it into position with the help of an assistant. If it feels likely to break, plane it down a little more. However, don't make the board any thinner than necessary. The stiffer the piece is, the better it will hold an even curve.

In most cases, a single thickness of fascia or skirting will be strong enough, especially if it is fastened to a framing member every 16 to 24 inches. If you need the additional strength of a second piece, laminate the two pieces using an exterior glue recommended for your area. You will need to clamp the piece frequently, nailing or screwing the second piece tight to the first.

Curved Horizontal Railing Pieces

To choose and plane boards for the curved railings, use the method described previously. However, you'll probably need to laminate two pieces together to create a strong, safe railing if you do much planing.

Measuring for curved sections in advance is almost impossible, so avoid cutting the lumber to length until after you've attached it. With one or two helpers, check carefully to see that the curve follows the contour of the deck. Then, fasten the rail to the posts using nails or screws.

Curved Railing

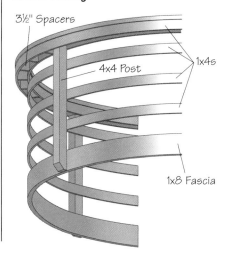

3½" Spacers

4x4 Post

1x4s

1x8 Fascia

Laminating the Railing Pieces.

To add a second board, you'll need lots of clamps. Allow one for every 4 to 6 inches. Use pads to ensure that your clamps won't mar the wood. Apply adhesive to the new piece, press it into place, and clamp it, making sure that all edges are flush. Allow the assembly to set overnight.

Making the Cap. To make the cap for this railing, cut pieces out of 2x12 or other appropriate width. Lay a 2x12 in place between posts, bend a piece of ¼-inch molding to approximate the curve, and mark the curve.

Don't throw away all the scrap lumber you produce. Use the cutout sections to fill in other parts of the curved piece as shown. Glue on slightly oversize pieces using a urethane glue, clamp them, and allow the glue to set completely. Then trim the glued-up piece to size.

To support the railing cap, install 3½-inch wide spacers as shown in the illustration "Curved Railing."

Creating Curved Caps

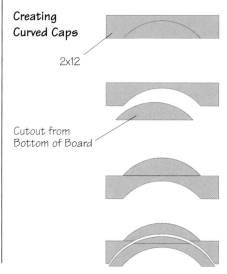

2x12

Cutout from Bottom of Board

Sheltered but Open

*T*he homeowners already had a simple deck in place when they called Marsh. What it needed most urgently was shelter from the elements. The deck sat above the treetops near the rim of a valley, which left it exposed to gusty winds that often made eating or lounging unpleasant. They also wanted some relief from the sun as well as a few design strokes that would relieve the deck's rectangular plainness.

On the other hand, the homeowners didn't want to give up their spectacular views. Marsh responded with a tempered-glass windbreak that surrounds about half of the deck's perimeter, a pergola that covers a third of its area, and some generously sized planters that bring color on board.

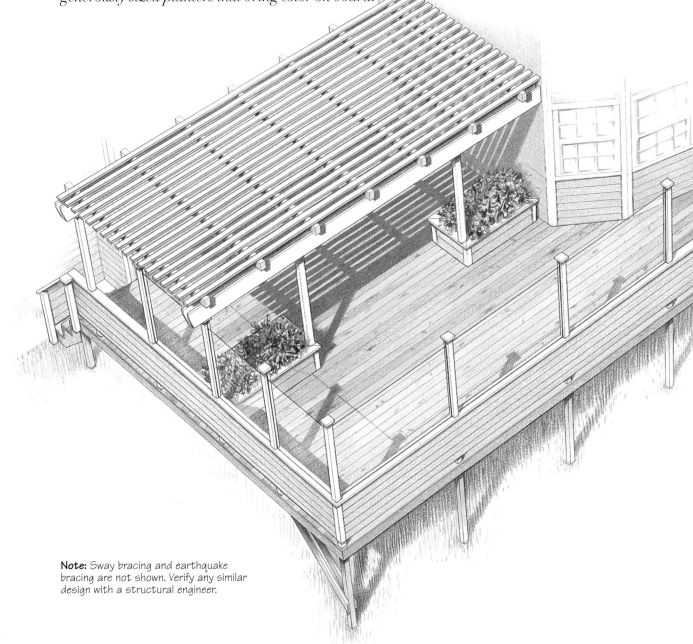

Note: Sway bracing and earthquake bracing are not shown. Verify any similar design with a structural engineer.

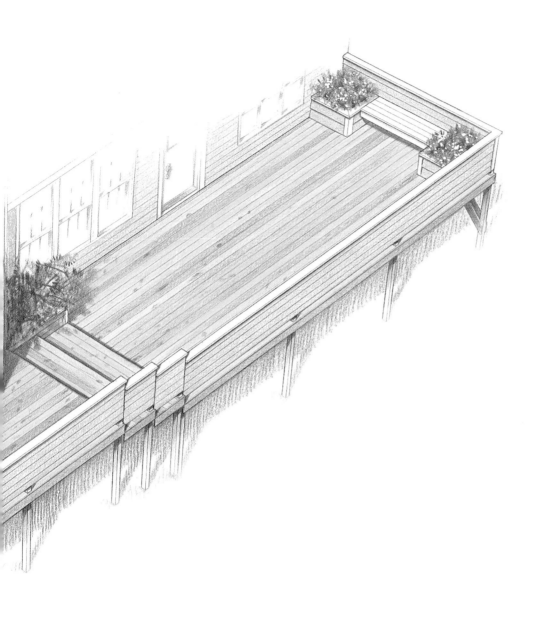

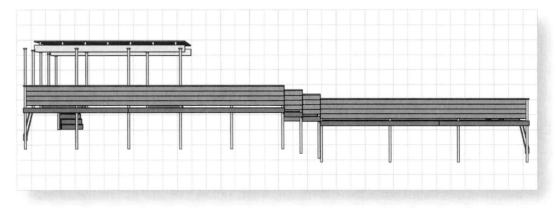

Ground View

Sheltered but Open, Plan View

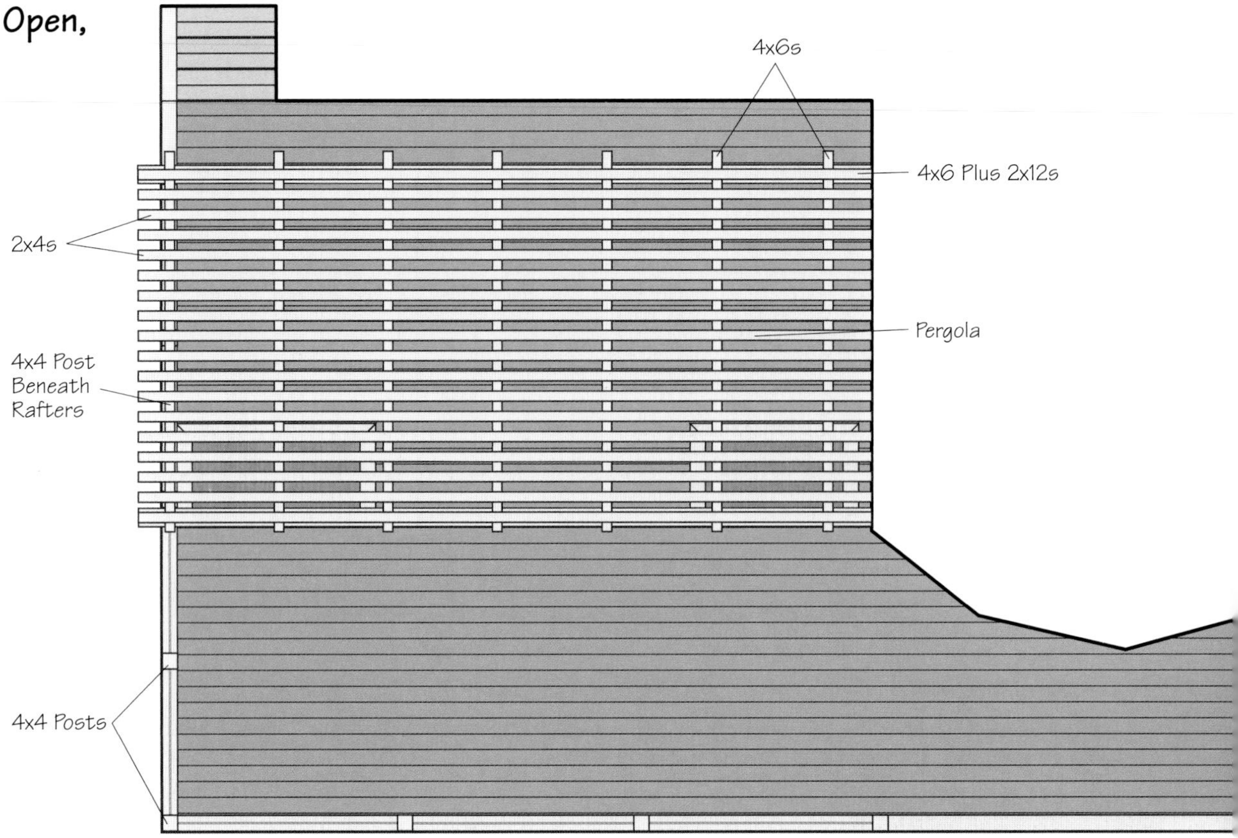

4x6s

4x6 Plus 2x12s

2x4s

Pergola

4x4 Post Beneath Rafters

4x4 Posts

Materials Used for This Deck

Framing (pressure-treated pine)	4x6s for beams 2x8 joists 2x8 ledgers and headers			2x6 seat pieces
Decking	2x6s		Pergola	4x4 posts 2x12s and 2x4s for beams 4x6s for top rafters 2x4s for top pieces
Fascia	1x8s			
Railing and windscreen	4x4 posts 2x6s for angled post braces 1x2 nailers to hold glass Sheets of ½"-thick tempered glass (check with local codes for required thickness) 8" beveled cedar siding Rough-sawn 1x4s for trim pieces		Hardware	3½" deck screws Joist hanger nails Post anchors for anchoring posts to concrete T-straps for tying beams to posts Joist hangers for 2x8s Angled joist hangers for 2x8s Angle brackets Lag screws with washers for anchoring the ledger and for angled post braces
Planters and bench	Galvanized sheet-metal liners, ordered to fit 2x4s for framing 8" beveled cedar siding Rough-sawn 1x4s for side and top trim pieces		Masonry	Concrete Precast concrete piers

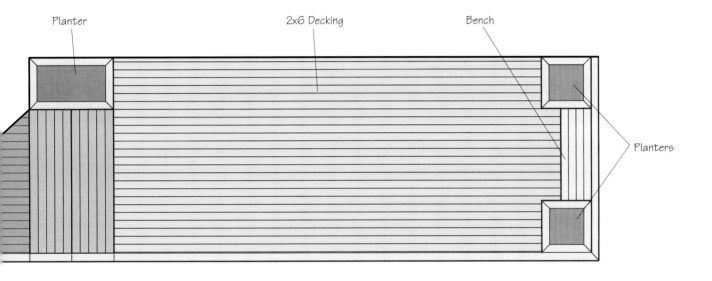

Planter   2x6 Decking   Bench   Planters

Pergola Elevation

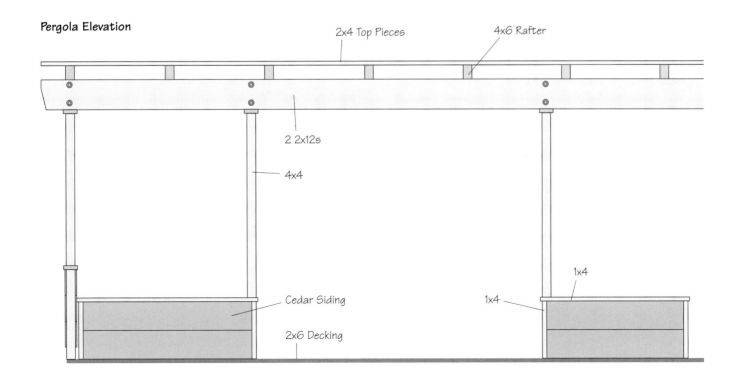

2x4 Top Pieces   4x6 Rafter

2 2x12s

4x4

Cedar Siding

2x6 Decking

1x4

1x4

Design Considerations

The existing deck on this site provided more than ample space for lounging and dining. In fact, it felt too roomy, and the lack of interesting angles or curves heightened the sense of bare expanse. A quick and obvious solution would have been to buy a large collection of patio furniture and add a few flowerpots. However, it's much easier to achieve a sense of harmony if you can build in elements that express themes and variations.

Blending Design

The house was covered with painted, rough-textured siding, and Marsh decided to continue that look throughout the deck. He covered the railings and planters with rough beveled siding and used rough-sawn material for the posts and beams of the pergola. In keeping with the straightforward design, Marsh used simple squares for the post caps. The closest thing to a flourish is the routed detail he added to the pergola's rafters.

Coping with Wind and Sun

As for the wind problem mentioned earlier, a simple solution proved best. On part of the deck, large panels of tempered glass span the distance from post to post. During times of high wind, this area provides comfort as well as unobstructed views. To enclose the entire deck with glass, however, would have transformed it into a room. This way, when the wind settles down, the rest of the deck still has the wide-open feel of an outdoor space.

With no tree cover, the deck sometimes got so hot that it radiated heat into the house itself, making it uncomfortably warm as well. The pergola covers the section of the deck that gets the most sun. By spacing 2x4s across the top at 7 inches on center (resulting in an interval that equals their width), Marsh achieved a pleasing symmetry as well as the right amount of shade.

The rough-hewn look of the planters complements that of the railings. Marsh equips the planters with galvanized sheet-metal liners and drain spouts that eliminate the possibility of overwatering.

Construction Techniques

If the site on which you're planning to build slopes severely, as this one does, hire a professional to install the footings.

The framing is straightforward. However, a heavy wind gust can exert a great deal of force on a large expanse of glass, so Marsh reinforced the posts for the windscreen with some sturdy bracing.

Cladding a Railing. A standard railing already existed, but Marsh encased it with siding and a top cap. With most railings, this is a simple enough job, but make sure you have adequate nailing surface for the siding at all points. For horizontal siding like this, you can simply nail directly to the posts and 2x4s that make up the railing. You may be able to butt the siding up against the cap; if not, you'll need to remove it. If the railing has balusters or rails that protrude beyond the plane of the posts, remove them as well.

Building the Overhead. As with most overheads, the pergola design looks more complicated than it actually is. The tricky part is to lift all those pieces before you've firmed up the structure. To do this, cut the posts to length and temporarily brace them in position. Construct the lower beams by sandwiching a 4x6 between two 2x12s.

Set the beams in place, and anchor them with bolts. To cut the grooves along both bottom edges and the ends of the 4x6 rafters, use a router with your choice of bit.

You might want to experiment with the top 2x4 pieces to determine how much shade a particular spacing will provide. For this design, Marsh used 2x4 scraps as spacers. To install the pieces, drive two deck screws at each intersecting joint.

Pergola Detail

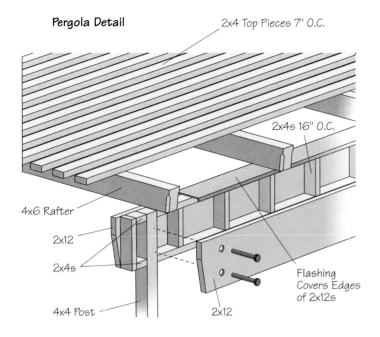

2x4 Top Pieces 7" O.C.

2x4s 16" O.C.

4x6 Rafter

2x12

2x4s

4x4 Post

2x12

Flashing
Covers Edges
of 2x12s

End-Wall Elevation (Looking Out)

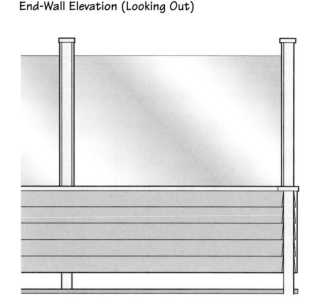

Constructing the Windscreen

If your area sustains high winds, consult the local building department for advice on how much bracing the windscreen will need. The angle brace shown is simple, but its triangular configuration is extremely strong. If the deck joists run parallel with the braces, align each post with one of the joists. Then, simply angle-cut 2x6s at 45 degrees on both ends; make the braces about one-fourth again as long as the vertical drop of the post. If the joists run perpendicular to the braces, install pieces of blocking that will provide solid anchor points for the braces. (See illustration.)

When you install the posts, double-check them to be sure they're plumb and to ensure that the openings will be square. The glass panes must fit securely.

Glass panes of this thickness cost a lot, so it's best to have the dealer install them. If they break a pane, you won't lose any money.

To install the glass yourself, nail the first set of 1x2s in place, and then test-fit the glass. Next, run a bead of silicone caulking along the 1x2, and set the glass in place. Run another bead of caulking along the edges of the glass; then immediately fasten the other 1x2s so that they firmly sandwich the pane.

End-Wall Elevation (Looking In)

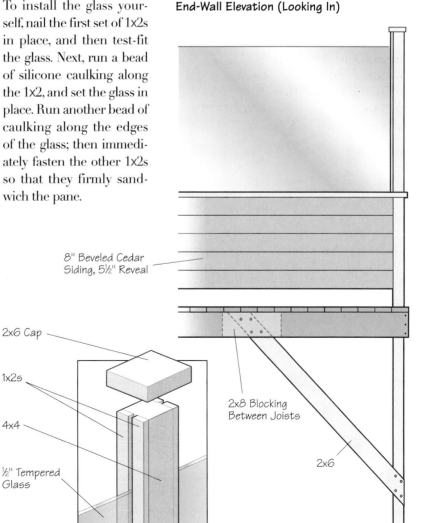

8" Beveled Cedar
Siding, 5½" Reveal

36"

2x6 Cap

1x2s

4x4

½" Tempered
Glass

2x8 Blocking
Between Joists

2x6

Shady Garden Spot

*B*esides an unobstructed view, the homeowners wanted a cozy getaway that would surround them with foliage. Oversize planters and an extensive overhead structure help make this deck a snug nest from which to view the world.

Note: Sway bracing and earthquake bracing are not shown. Verify any similar design with a structural engineer.

Outside View

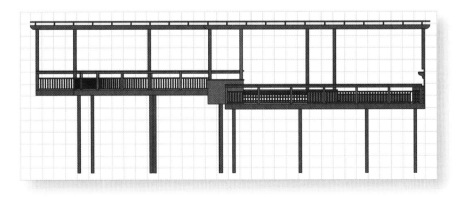

Design Considerations

Although the overhead structure shelters much of this deck, plenty of sunshine still gets through to keep plantings healthy. Because the deck faces south, its perimeter receives full sun for most of the day, making it a good location for flowerpots. Two gigantic planters are set back a bit, which gives them partial shade. Other areas get various amounts of sun, allowing the owners to choose a range of shade- and sun-loving plants.

A Gardener's Deck and More. This makes an ideal deck for a serious gardener who still enjoys comfort. A simple potting table located beneath the pergola features a sink with faucet and plenty of counter space. You can work in the heat of the day without breaking a sweat. If gardening is not your forte, the counter can be put to other uses or omitted.

The planters sit 2 feet above the deck surface, which saves the homeowners a good deal of back strain. At 4 feet square, they resemble small gardens that allow easy access from several sides.

Because dining usually takes place after the sun has sunk low, the eating area remains uncovered. The deck's only curved line helps to set this space apart, and the wide arc encourages diners to give the view a sweeping gaze.

From the eating area, you pass between large planters and down wide steps. One stairway descends toward the view, and a second, smaller set of steps leads to the work area and potting table. Benches set against the house also make this a pleasant place for a rest or chat.

Shady Garden Spot, Plan View

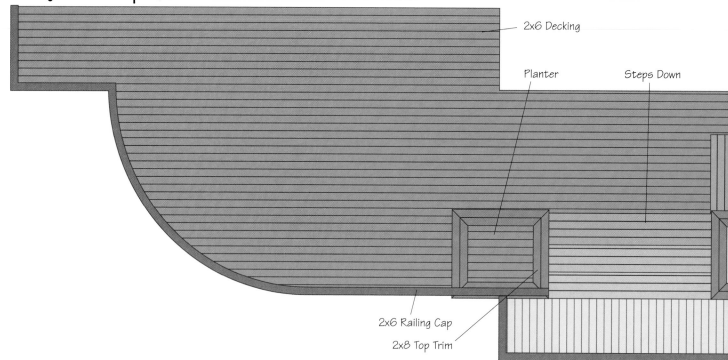

2x6 Decking

Planter

Steps Down

2x6 Railing Cap

2x8 Top Trim

Materials Used for This Deck

Framing (pressure-treated pine)	4x6 posts 4x12 beams 2x8s for joists, ledger, and blocking		Potting table	2x4s for framing 1x8s for trim and siding 2x8s for countertop 2x6s to frame around plumbing Plumbing materials for the faucet and small sink
Decking	2x6s		Bench	4x4 posts 2x4 framing 1x6 edging 2x6 seat pieces
Fascia	1x10s, planed as needed for the curve			
Railings	4x4 posts 2x4 rails 2x2 balusters 1x4s (2 pieces) for the top rail, planed for the curve 2x6 railing cap (cut from 2x12s for the curved section)		Trellis	One-by stock, ripped to ¾" wide
			Hardware	3½" deck screws and 1¾" deck screws Joist hanger nails Post anchors for anchoring posts to concrete T-straps for tying beams to posts Joist hangers for 2x8s Angle brackets Lag screws with washers for anchoring the ledger
Overhead	4x6 posts 2x8s for beams (2 pieces for each) 2x6 rafters 2x4 top pieces			
Planters	Galvanized liner, made to fit (4x6 overhead posts used for part of framing) 2x4s for framing 1x12s for side pieces 2x8s for top trim		Masonry	Concrete Reinforcing bar

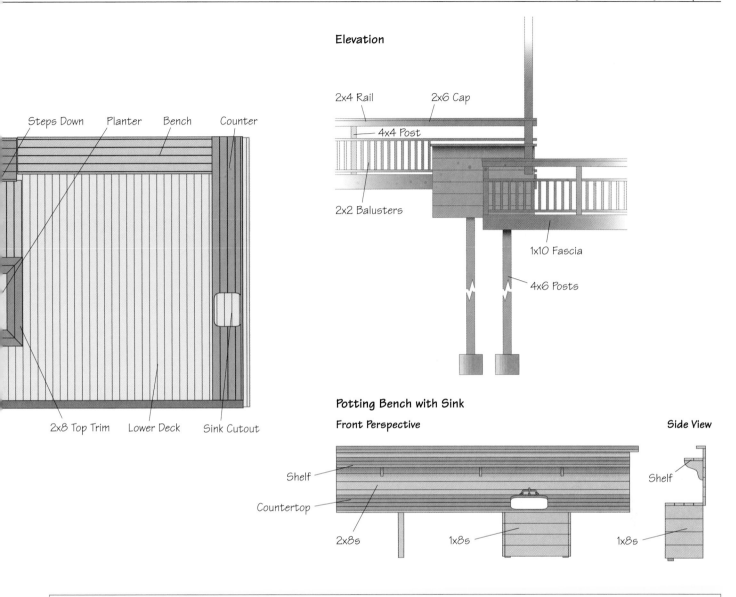

Elevation

2x4 Rail

2x6 Cap

4x4 Post

2x2 Balusters

1x10 Fascia

4x6 Posts

Steps Down   Planter   Bench   Counter

2x8 Top Trim   Lower Deck   Sink Cutout

Potting Bench with Sink

Front Perspective

Side View

Shelf

Countertop

Shelf

2x8s

1x8s

1x8s

Construction Techniques

This deck was built 12 feet above the ground, which explains the need for such massive beams and posts. The railing consists of 2x2 balusters and 2x4 rails. Two 1x4s serve as the top rail and support the 2x6 railing cap. To make the curved section of the railing, see page 129. If you plan to build planters as large as the ones shown here, you'll need to reinforce the framing beneath to support their weight. Add joists, or install extra support posts with footings.

Simple Trellis. To provide support for additional living greenery, Marsh erected an elegantly simple trellis and attached it to the house wall. To make the trelliswork, rip pieces of clear cedar one-by to ¾ inch wide. Arrange the pieces in a grid, and then check for squareness. Add short spacers to the back of the trellis to allow room for vines to climb. Drill a pilot hole, and drive a 1¾-inch screw into every joint. Attach the trellis to the wall using screws.

Trellis Detail

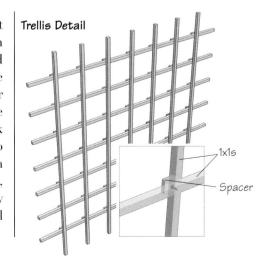

1x1s

Spacer

Soaking and Dining Areas with Shingled Siding

A *small deck with a hot tub already existed, but it didn't provide adequate room for dining and relaxing. The home-owners liked having the tub near the house, but the railing obstructed the view from tub level. Marsh solved this problem by building a new deck area three steps down from the tub and incorporating a glass panel into the railing.*

Outside View

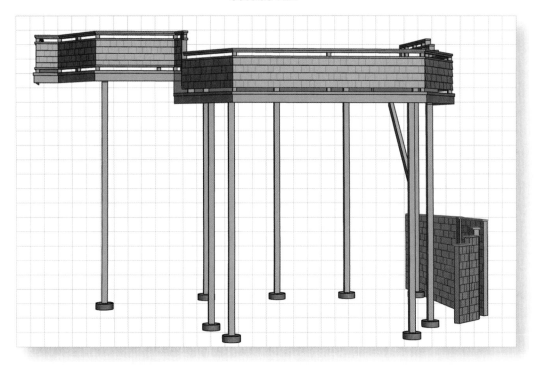

Note: Sway bracing and earthquake bracing are not shown. Verify any similar design with a structural engineer.

Soaking and Dining Areas with Shingled Siding, Plan View

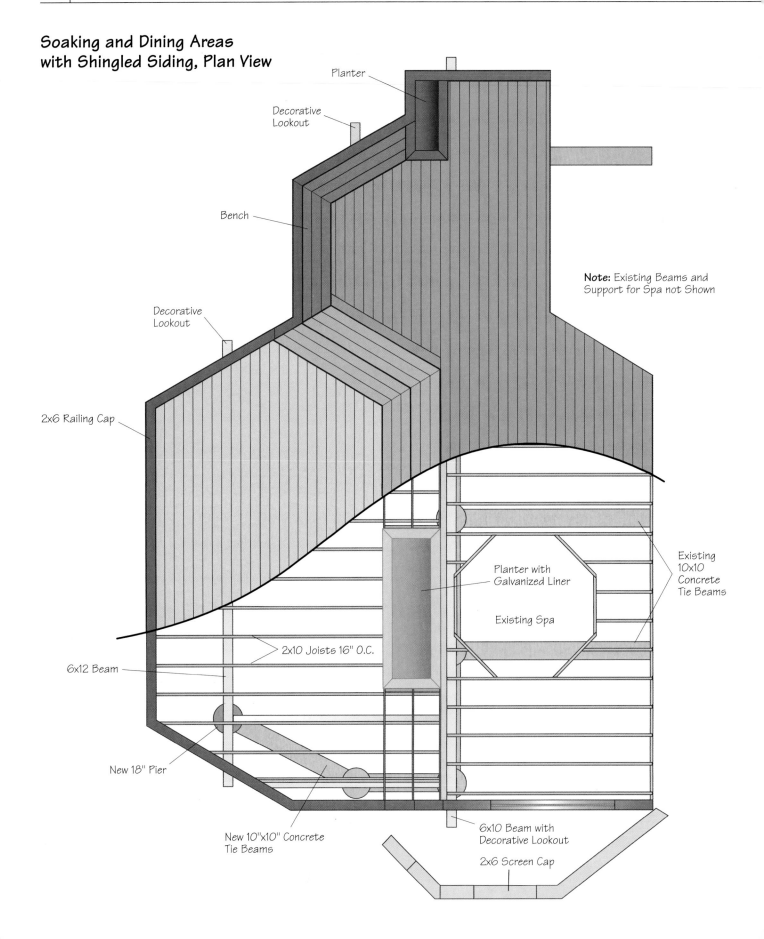

Planter

Decorative Lookout

Bench

Decorative Lookout

2x6 Railing Cap

6x12 Beam

New 18" Pier

New 10"x10" Concrete Tie Beams

2x10 Joists 16" O.C.

Note: Existing Beams and Support for Spa not Shown

Planter with Galvanized Liner

Existing Spa

Existing 10x10 Concrete Tie Beams

6x10 Beam with Decorative Lookout

2x6 Screen Cap

Side Elevation

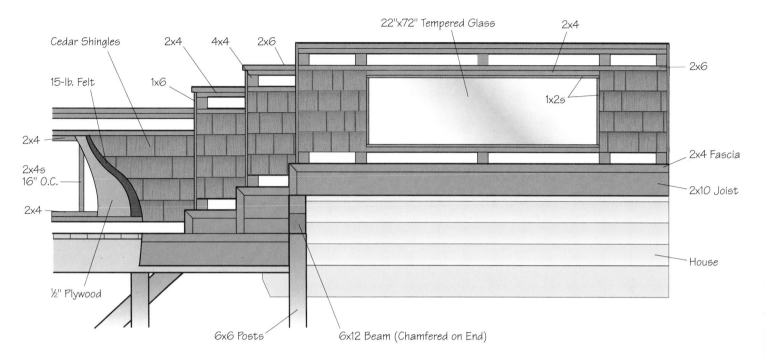

Cedar Shingles

15-lb. Felt

2x4

2x4s 16" O.C.

2x4

½" Plywood

2x4

1x6

4x4

2x6

22"x72" Tempered Glass

2x4

1x2s

2x6

2x4 Fascia

2x10 Joist

House

6x6 Posts

6x12 Beam (Chamfered on End)

Materials Used for This Deck

Framing (pressure-treated pine)	6x6s for posts 6x10s, 6x12s, and 4x10s for beams 2x10 joists 2x10 ledgers and headers			1x6s or cedar shingles for sides 1x2s for side trim
Decking	2x6s		Benches	4x4 posts 2x4 framing pieces 2x6 seat pieces
Fascia	2x4s and 1x6s (See rail detail.)		Hardware	3½" deck screws 4d nails for shingles Joist hanger nails Post anchors for anchoring posts to concrete T-straps for tying beams to posts Joist hangers for 2x10s Angled joist hangers for 2x10s Angle brackets Lag screws with washers for anchoring the ledger Lag screws with washers for angled post braces
Railings	4x4 posts 2x4 bottom and top rails and framing pieces 2x6 railing caps (one lower and one upper) 1x6s for vertical fascia pieces ½" CDX plywood 15-lb. roofing felt Cedar shingles ½" tempered glass (22"x72") 1x2s to hold the glass pane			
Planters	Galvanized sheet-metal liners, ordered to fit 2x4s for framing 2x6s for top trim		Masonry	Concrete Reinforcing bar

Design Considerations

The old deck's railing measured less than 2 feet from the hot tub, cramping guests as well as blocking their view. Because the tub is supported by a massive structure, moving it was out of the question. In addition, the homeowners liked having the tub nearer to the house than the dining area, simply because they did more soaking than outdoor dining.

Improving the View. On every deck that involves a railing, Marsh designs with the view in mind. In most cases, he has to consider several vantage points. Whether people are sitting on benches, looking out a kitchen or living-room window, or lounging in chairs, they prefer to look at the surroundings rather than the railings. To clear an obstructed view, Marsh often lowers all or part of the deck, as he did in this case. By dropping the deck area down three steps, Marsh was

able to increase its size as well as improve the view from the hot tub.

To further enhance the view, Marsh installed a tempered-glass panel in the railing where it comes closest to the tub level, allowing soakers to gaze at the countryside and some greenery. This panel opens up the view from the nearby bedroom window as well.

Other Considerations. Marsh also placed a large planter next to the tub on the panoramic view side, dropping it down a step so as not to create an obstruction. When filled with plants, it frames the view of the trees beyond with a foreground of foliage.

The lower deck is large enough that a table with chairs can be set off to one side where they won't hinder the view from the tub. Dropping this level down three steps from the tub's lofty height

also served to nestle the dining area pleasantly among the tops of the trees.

The railing and benches are sided with cedar shingles, the same material that covers the house. Lightly stained rather than painted, the shingles give the deck a warm, homey feel. However, too large an expanse of solid siding would make the railing seem massive, so Marsh added a 4-inch gap below the cap to open up the design.

As with most of his decks, Marsh installed low-voltage lighting at various points, especially on the step risers. Unless you have security concerns, bright floodlights usually detract from a deck's atmosphere. Multiple soft lights provide adequate illumination without the glare. Marsh finds that his clients often like to set the lights on timers so that the deck automatically becomes a part of their house at night.

Construction Techniques

For a severely sloped and elevated site like this one that calls for massive beams and posts, hire a professional to do the basic structural work, including the footings. If a deck like this is built near the ground, you can use standard footings, posts, and beams.

Railing with Shingles and Glassed Section

For a more enclosed feel, attach the 4x4 posts to the inside of the outside joist before installing the fascia and

decking, as shown in the railing diagram. Add three 2x4s that span from post to post and 2x4 studs every 16 inches on center. Cover the lower section with plywood, and install vertical 1x6 fascia pieces to provide surfaces against which the shingles can butt. Add the two 2x6 caps.

Before you install the cedar shingles, plan the job so that the reveal—the length of shingle left exposed—will measure the same on all courses. For the first (bottom) course, lay a straight board on top of the decking on which

the shingles can rest. Attach the shingles with 4d nails, leaving approximately a $\frac{1}{8}$-inch gap between shingles. On the first course only, install two layers so that all gaps will be covered. Snap chalk lines for the rest of the courses. Stagger the gaps so that none of the felt will be left exposed. You'll have to cut the top two courses to size.

For the glassed section, order a pane of $\frac{3}{8}$- or $\frac{1}{2}$-inch tempered glass to fit, leaving about $\frac{1}{8}$ inch to spare in width and length. Support the middle of the section by installing short lengths of 4x4, one between the decking and the bottom 2x4 and the other between the two 2x6 caps. Attach lengths of 1x2 around the outside perimeter of the opening, and cut matching pieces. Run a bead of clear silicone caulk along the inside of the 1x2, set the pane in place, run another bead of caulk, and install the other 1x2s to sandwich the glass.

Roundover Detailing. Using a router equipped with a roundover bit, you can add elegant details without much extra effort. Approach this task with care, however. Experiment on scrap wood to achieve the exact amount of rounding you want. Make sure the bit is sharp enough to cut cleanly without chipping.

If you wish to round-over the boards along their entire length, do so before you install each piece. If you prefer the effect shown in the illustration, rout after you've installed the pieces. The router base will stop you before you get to the end.

A More Finished Edge. In most cases, decking is simply allowed to overhang the edge of a deck or stairway by 1^1/$_2$ inches or so. If the cut ends of boards are visible, you get a rustic look.

However, you may want a more finished appearance, especially at the top of a stairway. (See "Step Detail," above right.) If so, consider the method shown. Here, Marsh has laid a piece of decking parallel to the edge of the deck, letting it overhang about an inch. He then butts the decking boards against it. This requires a good deal more work because each board must be cut to fit exactly. You may also need to add extra framing pieces to provide adequate surfaces for fastening all the decking.

Step Detail

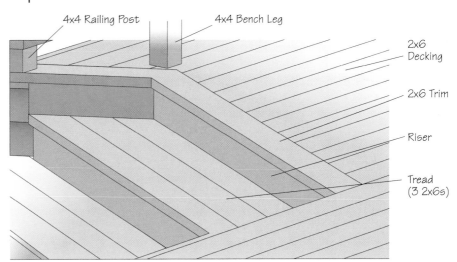

Glass Panel Installation

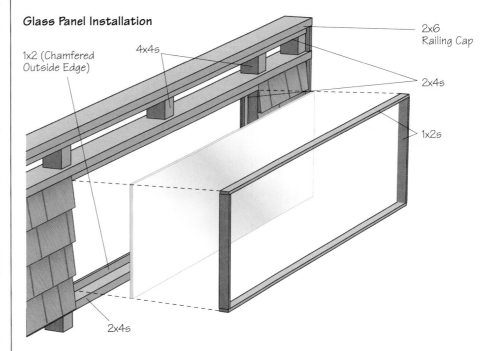

Railing Cap Detail

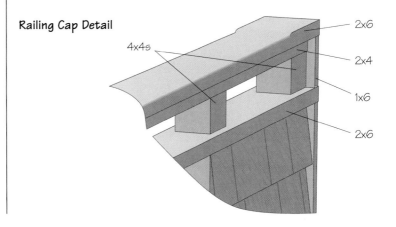

Square Corner with a Twist

*T*he homeowners wanted a deck with curved lines that would help to soften the house's rectangular shape. County setback requirements severely limited the distance that the deck could extend, especially at the corner. Marsh came up with an unusual orientation for this deck, which uses the house's corner to separate two functional areas.

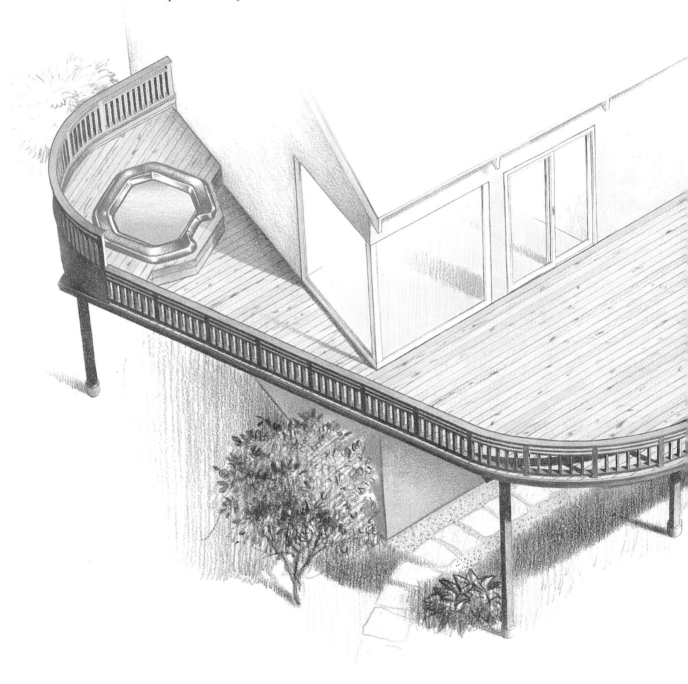

Note: Sway bracing and earthquake bracing are not shown. Verify any similar design with a structural engineer.

Design Considerations

It could be argued that this deck violates basic rules of design. It places curved lines starkly against a square-edged house. Its flowing contours contrast noticeably with the house's style (Tudor in this case). But keep in mind that design "rules" are guidelines, not laws. Don't be afraid to break them if you have good reason to do so, as in this case.

The house sits at an angle in relation to the property, which brings one corner to within 10 feet of the property line. With a 7-foot setback requirement, the deck could measure no more than 3 feet wide at that point. However, Marsh took that limitation and used it to advantage, creating a narrow "corridor" at that point that clearly separates two portions of the deck.

Found Space. Along much of its perimeter, the deck follows the line established by the setback to gain every possible inch of width. But the homeowners wanted style as well as size. By curving the edges of the two main areas, Marsh adapted the deck not to the house but to the hillsides onto which it looks. Though the shape may not correspond strictly to that of the house, it complements that of the landscape when you stand on the deck and gaze outward. That's what mattered most to the homeowners.

The smaller area provides just enough space for an average-size spa plus room for lounging on all sides of it. Soakers are fairly well secluded from the larger section. That larger side comfortably accommodates a table with chairs and still offers plenty of additional room for barbecuing, lounging, and arranging a brace of potted plants.

Marsh took advantage of a jog in the deck's perimeter by adding a section with an unusual J-shape bench. Here, guests can sit facing away from the house to admire the view, or they can cluster in the three-quarter circle to socialize.

Outside View

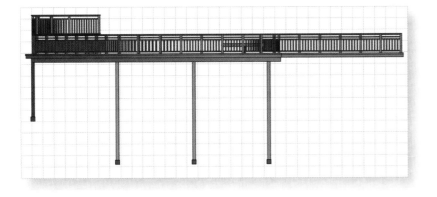

Square Corner with a Twist, Plan View

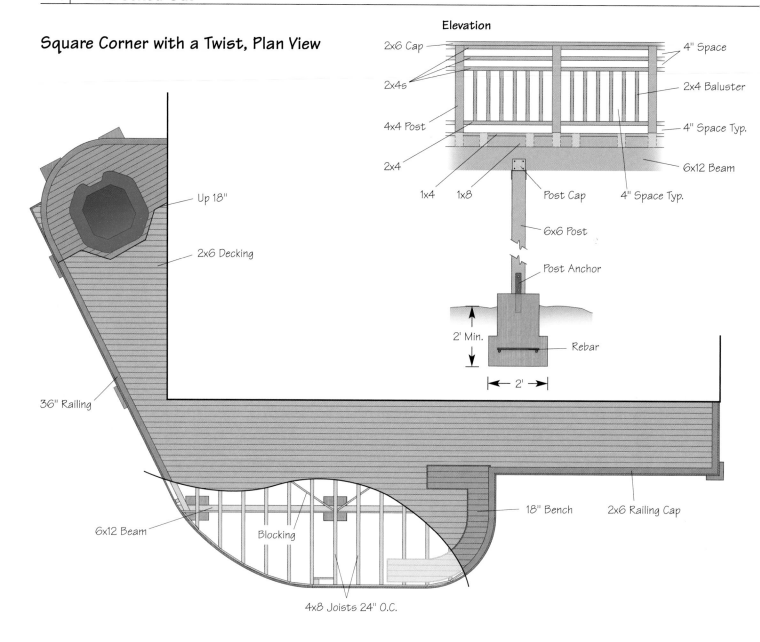

Elevation

2x6 Cap

2x4s

4x4 Post

2x4

1x4   1x8   Post Cap   4" Space Typ.

4" Space

2x4 Baluster

4" Space Typ.

6x12 Beam

6x6 Post

Post Anchor

2' Min.

Rebar

2'

Up 18"

2x6 Decking

36" Railing

6x12 Beam   Blocking

4x8 Joists 24" O.C.

18" Bench   2x6 Railing Cap

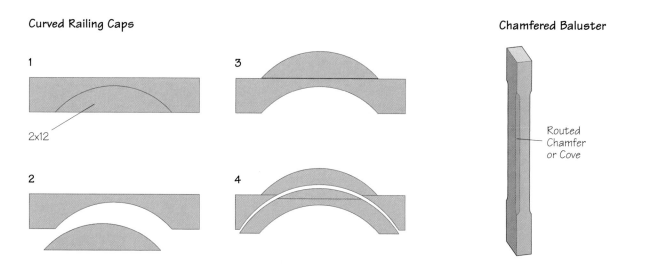

Curved Railing Caps

1

2x12

3

2

4

Chamfered Baluster

Routed
Chamfer
or Cove

Construction Techniques

Marsh often needs to support an elevated spa—a much more difficult job than setting one in the ground or on a concrete slab. For a large unit like this one, he uses 4x8 joists (spaced at 12 inches on center) that sit on 6x12 beams suported by 6x6 posts and large footings. Marsh spaces the 4x8 joists for the rest of the deck on 24-inch centers.

Railing with Chamfered Balusters

This substantial railing design calls for more pieces than most, but it's not terribly complicated to build, and it doesn't require advanced skills.

Install the posts first, and then cut the four 2x4 rails to fit between them. For the curved sections, cut the rails from 2x8s or 2x10s.

Marsh routed a pleasing chamfered detail on all four edges of the balusters. To add this profile, first cut the balusters to length (16½ inches); then set up a jig that will stop the router (equipped with a chamfer or cove bit) 2 inches from the ends of the boards. Rout the balusters all at one time, and then assemble the balustrade sections (balusters plus the two rails) before attaching them between the 4x4 posts. Toenail the balustrade front and back through the 2x4s. Then install the other 2x4 rails, toenailing them as well.

Curved Cap

To make the railing cap, use the method described in "Sweeping Elegance in a Small Space," on page 129 and illustrated at the bottom of the opposite page. Attach the caps to the posts, and then trim the edges in place using a roundover bit in a router. Rounding the edges not only reduces splinters and makes the railing more comfortable to hold, it reduces the apparent thickness of the cap, making it that much more aesthetically pleasing.

Materials Used for This Deck

Framing (pressure-treated pine)	6x6 posts 6x12 beams 4x8 joists 2x8 ledgers and headers		2x4s for framing 2x6s for seat 1x6s, planed where necessary for curved edging
Decking	2x6s	Hardware	3½" deck screws Joist hanger nails Post anchors for anchoring posts to concrete T-straps for tying beams to posts Joist hangers for 4x8s Angled joist hangers for 4x8s Angle brackets Lag screws with washers for anchoring the ledger
Fascia	1x8s and 1x2s, planed as necessary to make the curve		
Railings	4x4 posts 2x4 rails for the straight sections (four of them) 2x10s for curved rails (four of them) 1x6s (two pieces, laminated) for railing cap 2x4 balusters with chamfered edges		
		Masonry	Concrete Reinforcing bar
Bench	4x4 posts		

Stately and Symmetrical

he homeowners wanted a deck that would run along the entire 60-foot length of their house but wouldn't appear monstrous. They also wanted something a bit more formal than the usual deck. To create a stately but not massive look, Marsh designed a curved structure that evokes the shape of a grand piano and used turned and painted balusters in the railing to lighten its effect.

Note: Sway bracing and earthquake bracing are not shown. Verify any similar design with a structural engineer.

Design Considerations

Scientists claim that they can quantify beauty in human features: The more symmetrically aligned the eyes, nose, and mouth, the more beautiful (or handsome) the face appears to us. In a deck, however, symmetrical features often mean boring features. But if you start with interesting contours and want to maintain a formal aspect, symmetry may be the best way to go.

The master bedroom, dining and family rooms, and a second bedroom all look out onto the deck. However, the homeowners don't need to look downward to glimpse the treetops and adjacent bay, so Marsh didn't lower the deck as he typically would have.

What the owners now see is a railing with dignity. It features turned balusters that have been painted a classic white, and the railing cap has a round-over detail that you'd expect to see on fine furniture.

Symmetrical Design. The deck has a 16-foot semicircular bulge in its center that feels almost as if it were a ship's prow as you stand looking outward. It provides ample space for a large table and chairs. On both sides, the deck has rectangular sections that each measure about 8 feet wide—large enough for barbecuing, lounging, or dining at a small table.

To further enhance the sense of symmetry, Marsh arranged the diagonal decking boards to meet in the exact center without a divider board. This apparently simple touch requires a lot of meticulous work, but it gives the decking a finished feel like that of an interior floor.

Outside View

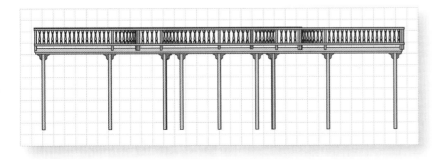

Stately and Symmetrical, Plan View

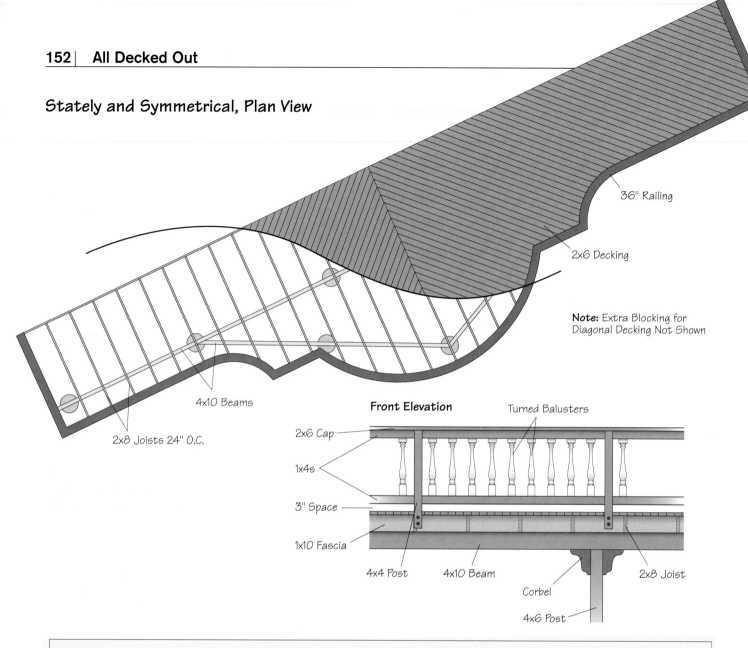

36" Railing

2x6 Decking

Note: Extra Blocking for Diagonal Decking Not Shown

4x10 Beams

2x8 Joists 24" O.C.

Front Elevation

Turned Balusters

2x6 Cap

1x4s

3" Space

1x10 Fascia

4x4 Post

4x10 Beam

Corbel

4x6 Post

2x8 Joist

Materials Used for This Deck			
Framing (pressure-treated pine)	4x6 posts 4x10 beams 2x8 joists 2x8 ledgers and headers Douglas Fir corbels for posts	Hardware	3½" deck screws 4" deck screws, for the railing Joist hanger nails Post anchors for anchoring posts to concrete T-straps for tying beams to posts Joist hangers for 2x8s Angled joist hangers for 2x8s Angle brackets Lag screws with washers for anchoring the ledger Carriage bolts for the railing posts
Decking	2x6s		
Fascia	1x10s, planed as necessary to make the curves		
Railings	4x4 posts 1x4s for top and bottom rails (planed for curved sections) Turned balusters, painted white 2x10s for curved railing cap sections 2x6s for straight railing cap sections	Masonry	Concrete Reinforcing bar

Construction Techniques

The sloped site and the deck's elevation called for large posts and beams as well as substantial footings. If your project presents similar challenges, it's best to hire a professional to install the footings and understructure. On a more conventional site, standard structural elements will do. To build the curved fascia and railing cap, see "Sweeping Elegance in a Small Space," page 129, and other of Marsh's decks.

Decking That Meets in the Middle

This feature is trickier to achieve than it appears. If this exact look—diagonally cut boards that butt directly against each other—isn't important to you, then run a divider board down the middle and butt the boards against it. (See "Getting It All in a Small Space," page 92.)

Choose dry, stable lumber. Avoid boards with hairline cracks near the ends (known as checking), or plan to cut off these areas, as they will probably enlarge over time. Also, measure all boards for width. They often vary by as much as 1/16 inch, which can cause serious misalignment in this arrangement. Butt together only boards of identical widths.

Plan Ahead. Prepare for the diagonal decking detail at the time you do the framing. Install joists and blocking that will provide ample nailing surfaces for the decking. Try to avoid having to drive nails or screws within 1 1/2 inches of the end of any decking board.

When you install the decking, allow plenty of time to get it right. Begin near the middle of the run rather than at either end. Check your 45-degree cuts carefully for accuracy, and lay out the first boards exactly perpendicular to each other and at a 45-degree angle to the house. You'll need to make small adjustments as you go in order to keep the butt joints aligned and the gaps between decking boards consistent.

Roundover Detail on the Railing Cap. This profile looks elegant and requires little extra work. Fit your router with a roundover bit, and adjust it to cut only a partial profile. Experiment on scrap lumber until you get the desired look—a 1/8-inch lip at the bottom is a good choice. Once you've cut each railing-cap piece to width and length, rout along both top edges, and then install it.

Curved Railing with Turned Balusters. Choose milled balusters that appeal to you, and give them

several coats of exterior white paint. You'll find this much easier that trying to paint them after you've completed the railing.

Once you've installed the railing posts, attach two lengths of 1x4 to their house side, one of them flush with the post tops and the other with its bottom edge about 1/2 inch lower than the planned bottom of the balusters. For the curved sections, plane the 1x4s until they are just flexible enough to make the curves. Then install the railing cap. To ensure a finished look on the inside of the railing, drill pilot holes, and drive screws through the posts from the outside and into the railing cap and 1x4s.

Attach the balusters, spacing them evenly between the railing posts and butting them up to the railing cap. Next, cut lengths of 1x4 for the other face of the "sandwich" at the bottom. Attach the 1x4s to the posts and balusters.

Railing Detail

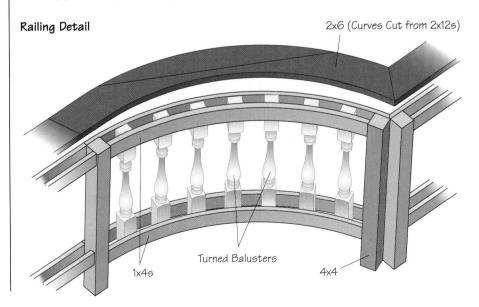

2x6 (Curves Cut from 2x12s)

1x4s

Turned Balusters

4x4

Promenade
with Circular Viewing Area

*M*arsh's clients in this case owned a newer home that was set on a severely inclined slope. This factor limited the overall size of the deck, but with the house's modern styling, Marsh felt free to choose almost any shape. The solution he came up with has a pleasantly straightforward look and a distinctive metal railing that doesn't obstruct the view.

Outside View

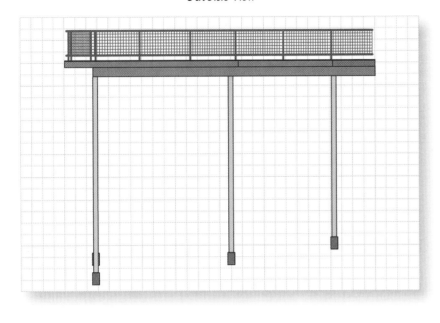

Note: Sway bracing and earthquake bracing are not shown. Verify any similar design with a structural engineer.

Design Considerations

The house has clean, spare lines and floor-to-ceiling glass walls that allow the homeowners to gaze out over the treetops to the bay below. They wanted a deck that would wrap around the house to provide a view from two sides, something the existing deck didn't offer. The existing conventional wooden railing also blocked the limited view it did provide.

The homeowners didn't need a large space, nor were they interested in the usual cooking and dining areas. They did, however, want to link their home more effectively to the outdoors, so Marsh designed a promenade of sorts—wide enough for strolling and placing potted plants with a larger area in the middle for engaging in conversation.

An Eye to the View. With a deck that measures only 8 feet wide in most places, it wouldn't make sense to step the structure downward to improve the view. Each step would eat up at least a foot of usable width.

Instead, Marsh designed a railing that, safe and sturdy though it is, barely seems to exist as you look through it. Made of steel and anodized dark green to blend with the leaves just beyond it, the structure has a contemporary Euro look, but its color and curving contour give it an organic feel. As a complement to this, the glass walls create an unusual relationship between the deck and the house. From certain angles, the decking appears to be an extension of the interior floor rather than a separate space.

Promenade with Circular Viewing Area, Plan View

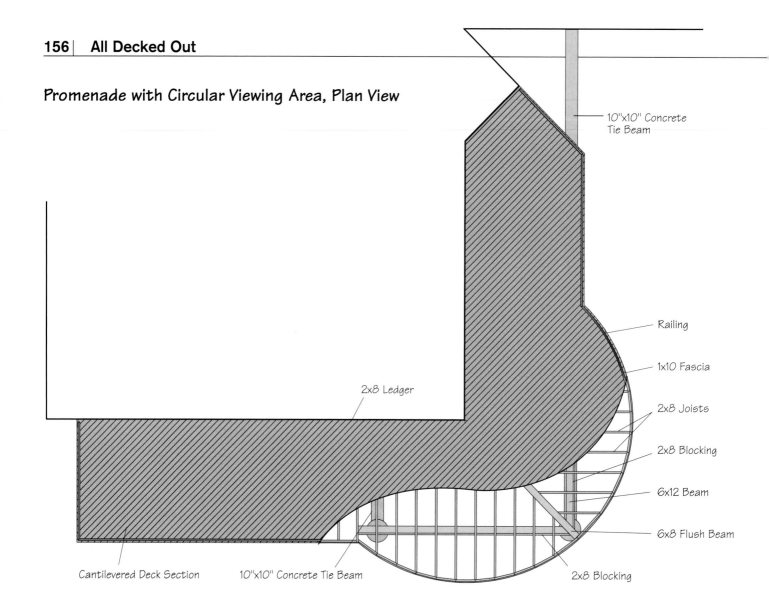

10"x10" Concrete Tie Beam

Railing

1x10 Fascia

2x8 Joists

2x8 Blocking

6x12 Beam

6x8 Flush Beam

2x8 Ledger

Cantilevered Deck Section

10"x10" Concrete Tie Beam

2x8 Blocking

Materials Used for This Deck			
Framing (pressure-treated pine)	6" steel posts 6x12 beams 6x8 flush beam 2x8 joists 2x8 ledgers and headers	Hardware	2" deck screws Joist hanger nails Post anchors for anchoring posts to concrete Joist hangers for 2x8s Angled joist hangers for 2x8s Angle brackets Lag screws with washers for anchoring the ledger Stainless-steel lag screws for attaching the railing
Decking	1x6 hardwood		
Fascia	1x10s, planed as necessary to make the curves		
Railing (all steel anodized green and welded together)	2" steel pipe for the rails 1½" steel pipe for the posts ¼" steel plates welded to the posts, for attaching to the framing & house Welded wire mesh made of ¼" steel in a 4" square pattern	Masonry	Concrete Reinforcing bar

Construction Techniques

Side Elevation

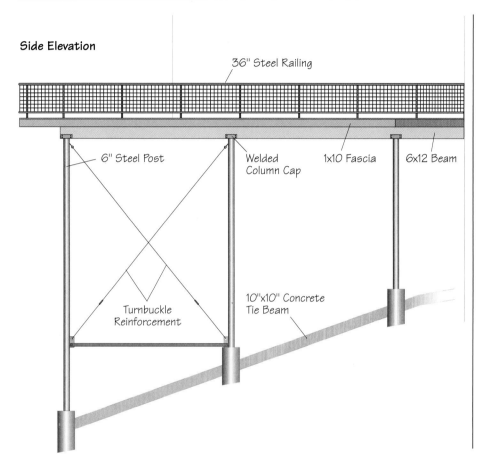

36" Steel Railing

6" Steel Post

Welded Column Cap

1x10 Fascia

6x12 Beam

Turnbuckle Reinforcement

10"x10" Concrete Tie Beam

Steel Railing

Few homeowners—or even professional carpenters—will have the skills and equipment needed to build a railing like this. The best approach is to construct the framing and then call in a local metalworking company to build the railing to your specifications. This will cost a good deal, but it's the only safe and practical way to get the job done. **Note:** Check with your local building department first. Some codes may specify a smaller-grid steel mesh to prevent small children from climbing the railing.

If you'd prefer to conceal the metal plates and bolt heads, arrange for the fencing company to secure the railing to the inside face of an outside joist at corners. This method may, however, require that you install extra framing pieces.

Marsh encountered a formidable challenge in installing the footings for this deck. He sank 18-inch-diameter concrete footings 6 feet into bedrock and tied all footings to each other and to the house with massive steel-reinforced concrete beams. The structural members—6-inch steel posts and 6x12 beams—had to be lifted over the house and into place using a crane. This is definitely a job for a professional.

The techniques used here can be found on some of Marsh's other decks. For instructions on building the curved fascia, for example, see page 129.

Railing Detail

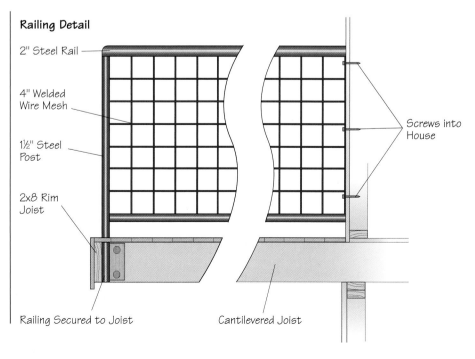

2" Steel Rail

4" Welded Wire Mesh

1½" Steel Post

2x8 Rim Joist

Screws into House

Railing Secured to Joist

Cantilevered Joist

Decks Appeal

Rick Parish
Decks Appeal
Plano, Texas
972/964-8821

Rick Parish of Decks Appeal, located near Dallas in Plano, Texas, is one of the few deck builders in the country to have his own showroom. There you'll see deck samples that show some of his signature design elements, as well as outdoor furniture pieces made to blend well with the decks. By spending all of his time meeting with customers and

▲ **Rick Parish uses redwood** in most of his decks, as evidenced by this fine example.

▶ **Interesting angles** and decorative design elements are part of Parish's design arsenal.

designing decks, Parish keeps three or more construction crews busy. He starts by listening to the homeowners to get a sense of how they intend to use their deck and how they envision its general contours.

Design Considerations

Parish finds that most of his clients have few specific ideas of their own and so look to him for design concepts. While he takes measurements, he has them glance through his impressive portfolio. Often they'll say "We want a deck just like that one," but Parish encourages them to let him design a deck that suits their individual needs. He then retires to the solitude of his office, where he uses computer design programs as well as pencil and paper to sketch a first idea. When he presents this first drawing to the homeowners, ideas come forth, leading to the second and usually final drawing.

Material of Choice

Parish uses Construction Heart, or Con Heart, redwood for nearly every exposed surface on his decks. This knotty material costs a good deal more than pressure-treated lumber but quite a bit less than clearer grades of redwood. Con Heart offers most of the advantages of more expensive redwood. It is less apt to splinter than pressure-treated pine, it resists shrinkage and twisting, and it has natural good looks. In fact, Parish has found that many homeowners prefer the rustic appearance of the knottier Con Heart to the smoother grain of clear lumber.

Using this material, however, requires more careful selection and planning. Before you buy, inspect the boards for loose knots that will likely fall out in a year or two. Also, plan your cuts carefully to avoid leaving half a knot at the end of a board. Lastly, this lumber tends to be a bit rougher, so make sure you sand pieces that will be handled, such as rails and tabletops.

Environmental Concerns

Sun. From years of experimenting in harsh Texas sunlight, Parish has learned that decks should be stained annually, or at least every other year. Most folks in his area don't like the looks of a deck that has gone gray.

A deep reddish-brown seems to harmonize better with the colors of the land as well as the tastes of Southwesterners. Decks Appeal offers its own brand of stain, a standard oil-based product reinforced with water sealers and blended to this color. In Parish's experience, oil-based stain-sealers last much longer than water-based products.

For fasteners, Parish uses double-coated screws that are first galvanized and then ceramic-coated. The hot Dallas summers will often pull nails out, but Parish has found that $2\frac{1}{2}$-inch screws (driven at least 1 inch into joists) will hold. The double-dipping ensures that the heads will never rust, at least in his area.

More often than not, Parish's clients want an overhead structure to go along with their deck. This provides filtered shade without restricting air movement as a solid roof would.

Soil. The soil in the Dallas area is notorious for its instability. Driveways and pools sometimes sink a foot or more within a short period of time. For this reason, Parish never attaches a deck to the house with a ledger board. If the deck (or the house) were to sink, it could seriously damage both structures.

▼ *This raised deck is a good example of Parish's penchant for curves.*

Overhead structures (above and below) are important features on most of Parish's decks. They provide dappled shade for most of the day in the sunny Southwest.

Techniques to Use

Many of Parish's designs are less complicated than they look. He often achieves an appearance of furniture-like detailing by adding simple pieces. However, such detail work requires precise cuts in order to look good. For this purpose, you should consider a quality power miter saw (chop saw) a necessity rather than a luxury.

▶ Much of the distinctive look of Parish's decks comes from his materials. After carefully selecting dark-colored Con Heart boards that have no loose knots, he chooses the best pieces for the most visible elements of the deck.

▶ His post design adds elegance without requiring a lot of work. By attaching 2x2s that run up the center of each face of a standard 4x4, he creates a classically fluted column. He also installs banding at the top of each post made of 2x2s and ripped 2x4s, although this detail requires careful cutting and fastening.

▶ In his designs, Parish avoids butt joints in the decking, which tend to mar its unbroken appearance. This sometimes means dividing a large deck into smaller sections. He's rarely found a good reason to make a deck surface that measures more than 20 feet (the longest standard decking length) in both directions. Though butt-jointed decking can look fine if you prefer a rustic look, avoid it if you want a more finished appearance.

▶ Not only does Parish recommend regular staining to reduce the punishing effects of sunlight, he also urges customers to avoid damaging their decks with furniture and pots. For instance, by using simple trivets made from 2x2s to hold flowerpots off the deck, they can prevent water stains and scratches. (See "Curves and More Curves," page 179.)

▶ If a deck has gone gray due to neglect, Parish cautions against using a high-pressure washer. These machines, which are sold in home centers and touted as cure-alls for wood surface problems, may actually do more harm than good. On softwoods such as redwood, they can remove the soft part of the grain, leaving a rough surface that can be made smooth again only through heavy sanding. Instead, he recommends a two-step solution: First, spray or sponge on a 50-50 mixture of household bleach and water, which will make the gray disappear almost immediately. Rinse and then brush the deck with a mixture of oxalic acid (wood bleach) and water. This will leave you with a deck that is nearly white. Apply stain, and the wood will look like new.

▶ Parish designs overhead structures, or pergolas, carefully to provide the desired amount of shade. He runs the top slats, usually 2x2s, in a north-to-south direction so that the sun can shine directly between them only at noon. In the Dallas area, he's found that 2x2s laid 3 inches on center (spaced $1^{1}/_{2}$ inches apart) provide full shade for an hour or two (in the morning on an east-facing deck and in the evening on a west-facing deck). For the rest of the day, the overhead structure will provide filtered shade of varying degree. This much planning may sound complicated, but it will increase the utility of your deck and save work in the long run.

▶ Parish uses a lot of curves, not only on his decks and railings but sometimes on overhead structures as well. (See "Pagoda Platform," page 180.) To the homeowner, curves can look daunting, like something better left to a professional. They also cost more in materials; you often need to start with a 2x12 and then waste nearly half of the board. But if you have a professional-grade saber saw and the patience to do things right, you can add impressive-looking curves to your project.

▶ Parish uses a router fitted with a roundover bit to create the finished look of his decks, usually following up with a sander. If you take some time beforehand to practice your routing on scrap material, you'll find that you can get the near-furniture-quality results you see in his work. Unless you have a lot of experience with a belt sander, however, use this tool with great caution and only with fine-grit sandpaper. It removes wood very quickly and can leave gouges and other blemishes that can't be repaired.

▼ *The deep reddish brown color* of this deck is typical of those Parish builds and stains.

Freestanding Deck with Spa and Fire Pit

his deck may be small, but it has lots of flair. Kids and adults can sit around the fire pit and roast marshmallows, then hop into the spa. It almost reminds you of summer camp.

Ground View

Design Considerations

With decks that sit low above the ground like this one, you don't have to worry about space for parties. When guests show up for the occasional large get-together, they can simply spill over onto the lawn if need be. For the rest of time, this design provides plenty of room for cozy get-togethers—family lounging, barbecuing, and soaking, as well as gathering around the fire.

Parish surrounded the spa with just enough decking so that guests could sit and dangle their legs. (The spa cover, which gets stowed next to the house, doesn't require deck space.) The unit sits three levels up from grade, or about 21 inches. Parish finds that this height makes spa installation easier. (See Construction Techniques, page 167.)

A railing runs around one-half of the spa, more for privacy rather than safety. The balusters are self-spaced; that is, the gaps between them measure the same width ($1^1/2$ inches) as the 2x2 balusters themselves. A "railing" that leads up to the spa actually serves as a towel rack, with two horizontal rails made of rounded 2x2s.

About 5 feet from the spa, a brick fire pit rises about 8 inches above the decking. The pit is not intended for cooking—a conventional grill works better—but it makes an ideal place to gather after supper. With a crackling fire, relaxed conversation naturally takes place. A bench curves halfway around the pit, facing toward the spa.

The first level measures about 12 feet square, allowing enough room for a dining table and cooking area. In one corner, a triangular opening makes a distinctive spot for planting flowers or a small shrub. In fact, angles tend to dominate throughout, giving the deck a pleasantly jumbled look. The assortment of odd angles showcases the spa and fire pit, both of which are octagonal.

**Freestanding Deck with
Fire Pit and Spa, Plan View**

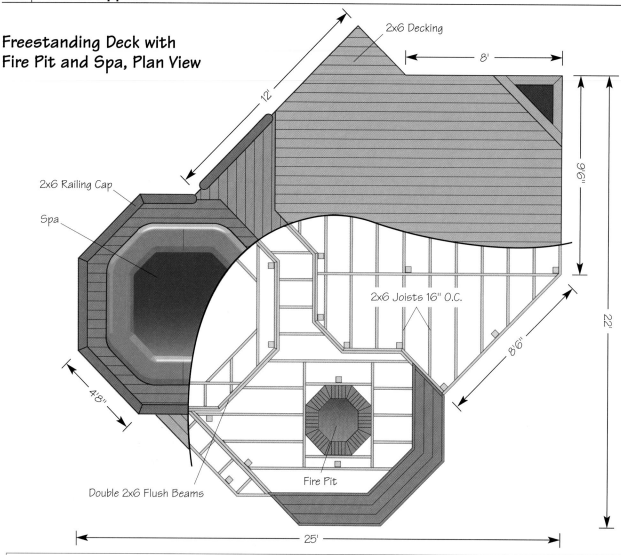

2x6 Decking

8'

2x6 Railing Cap

Spa

9'6"

2x6 Joists 16" O.C.

22'

8'6"

4'8"

Double 2x6 Flush Beams

Fire Pit

25'

Materials Used for This Deck

Framing	4x4 posts Doubled 2x6s for flush beams 2x6 joists		Hardware	Joist hangers for 2x6s Angled joist hangers for 2x6s Angle brackets Fasteners for joist hangers 3" deck screws 3" lag screws with washers for bench posts 2½" deck screws
Decking	2x6s			
Bench	4x4 posts 2x6 seat pieces 2x4 framing 2x4 trim for bottom of posts			
			Masonry	Bricks, fire bricks, and mortar for fire pit Sand to support spa Reinforcing bar for fire-pit foundation Concrete Concrete tube forms or lumber for building forms Solid concrete blocks for footings
Railing	4x4 posts 2x4 top and bottom rails 2x2 balusters 2x6 railing cap			
Railing/ towel rack	4x4 posts 2x2 rails (bars) 2x6 railing cap			

Construction Techniques

Side Elevation

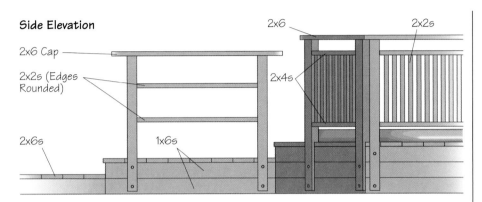

2x6 Cap

2x2s (Edges Rounded)

2x6s

1x6s

2x6

2x2s

2x4s

A low-to-the-ground deck usually leaves no room for a beam under the joists, so take the time to accurately lay out the many footings that directly support the joists. If local codes allow, dig your footing holes, position the posts, and build the framing before you pour the concrete.

Supporting a Spa with Washed Sand

Parish prefers the technique that follows, but check with your building department before you try it. Local codes may require you to pour a concrete foundation.

After you've completed the framing, but before you lay the decking, dig a hole for the spa. In this case, the top of the 36-inch-deep spa sits 21 inches above grade. The hole should allow about a foot of clearance below the bottom of the spa, so dig the hole approximately 27 inches deep—not a big job.

Tamp the soil at the bottom of the hole; then shovel in and level a foot or so of sand. Set temporary 2x6 blocks on top of the framing to index the future thickness of the decking, and set the spa on top of them, resting its lip directly on the blocks. Shovel sand into the hole until it fully supports the spa.

Now comes the interesting part of the job. Fill the spa halfway with water. Using a garden hose, soak the sand fully to compact it. Add more sand, and then soak it again if necessary. The moisture-compacted sand will form a firm base that will support the spa for decades.

Fire Pit

Unless you have a fair amount of masonry experience, you'd do well to hire a professional mason to build the pit. An octagon poses a serious challenge to the beginner. To start, frame a square hole large enough so that the firebricks will not directly touch the wood. If possible, build the pit before you lay the decking; this work can easily scratch the wood.

At the bottom, excavate a foundation hole if necessary, so the fire pit ends up about 18 inches deep. (The foundation should measure 3 to 4 inches in depth.) Pour a steel-reinforced concrete pad that measures a few inches larger than the pit's diameter. From the foundation, lay firebricks in an octagonal shape to a height of 4 to 6 inches above the decking surface. Cover the firebrick with natural brick, making the total structure about 8 inches higher than the decking.

Fire Pit Detail

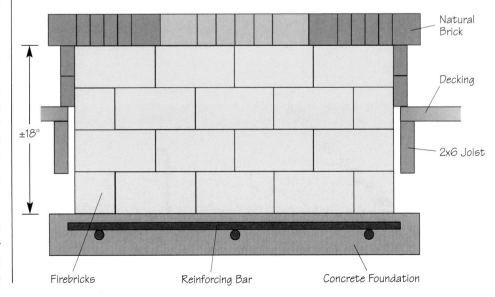

Natural Brick

Decking

2x6 Joist

±18"

Firebricks

Reinforcing Bar

Concrete Foundation

Circular Eating Area

Here's a bit of whimsy: a round platform, just the right size for a table with chairs, that can be set on top of a deck or patio. The railing is just for looks, while the benches provide a comfortable conversation area.

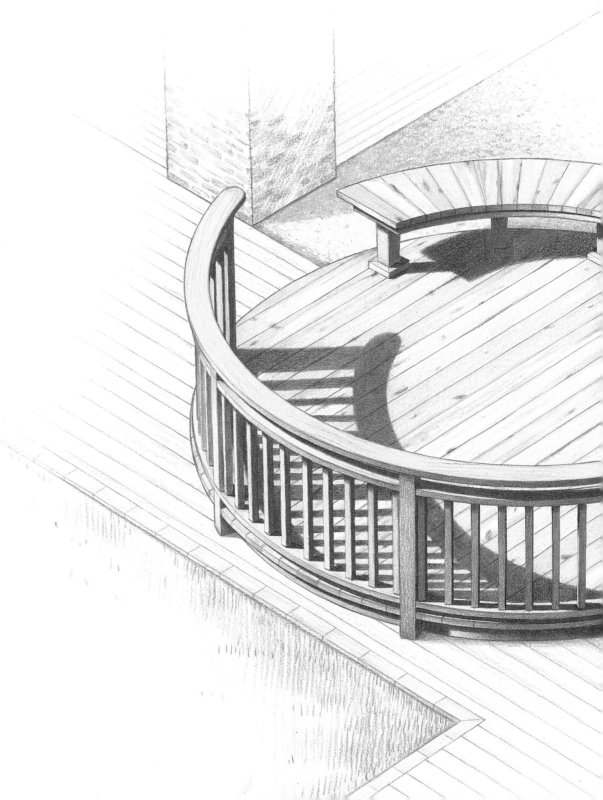

Ground View

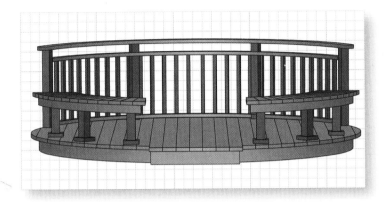

Design Considerations

This little deck offers just enough space for a circular patio table with chairs, plus room for a server to walk around the chairs while people are eating. Whenever you plan an eating area such as this one, with clearly defined borders, first test the dimensions by setting your furniture in place to find out how much room you'll really need.

Although not a safety requirement here, the railing gives the little deck a sense of enclosure. Leaning on it as they look toward the pool, adults can easily keep an eye on the kids—while the railing is there to remind the children that this is adult space.

Parish positioned the benches to the rear of the deck and behind the railing, creating a semi-secluded conversation area. The benches' curved shape makes for good groupings. People are forced to look neither at nor away from each other.

Circular Eating Area, Plan View

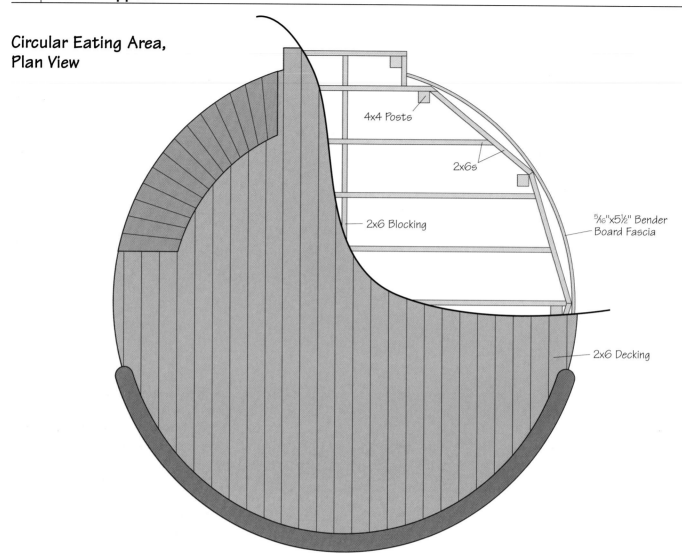

4x4 Posts

2x6s

2x6 Blocking

⁵⁄₁₆"x5½" Bender Board Fascia

2x6 Decking

Materials Used for This Deck and Overhead

Framing	4x4 posts (not needed if you're building on an existing deck or patio) 2x6 joists		Benches	2x4 top pieces 4x4 posts 2x4 framing pieces ⁵⁄₁₆"x3½" bender board, ripped from 2x4s 2x6s for seat pieces
Decking	2x6s			
Fascia	⁵⁄₁₆"x5½" bender board, ripped from 2x6s		Hardware	Joist hangers for 2x6s Angled joist hangers for 2x6s Fasteners for joist hangers 3" deck screws 2½" deck screws Carriage bolts with washers and nuts for rail posts
Railing	4x4 posts 2x4 rails cut out of 2x8s 2x2 balusters 2x6 railing cap cut out of 2x12s			
Overhead	4x4s for posts (four for each post) 2x8s for beams (two for each beam) 4x6 rafters			

Construction Techniques

If the circular deck is not resting on a solid surface, you'll need to pour numerous footings for such a small space. The impressive benches and railing will both take time to build, but a patient do-it-yourselfer can handle the job without much difficulty.

Building a Low Circular Deck

Start by making an X with three lengths of 2x6: one that spans the length of the deck and two half-long pieces running perpendicular to it that are attached to its center. Check for squareness. Cut the outside pieces. There are ten sides, all of which should measure the same length. Miter-cut the ends of each piece at 18 degrees (leaving you with a 72-degree complementary angle). For a 10-sided frame that measures 10 feet in diameter, cut each piece to 38 inches finished length.

Now, locate the corner points for the framing (10 in all, plus two for the noncircular "landing" section) by measuring from the center of the X and using the outside pieces as guides.

Fasten the pieces together using temporary cleats on top. Measure the diameter across all five pairs of parallel sides, and adjust them so that they come out pretty even. They needn't be perfect. Install posts and footings, if required. If you're building on top of a solid surface, use shims to raise the joists ¼ inch or so to allow the framing to dry out after a rain. Now, fill in the rest of the framing.

Install the posts for the benches, anchoring them securely to the framing. Next, install the decking, allowing it to run wild. Attach a 5-foot 1½-inch string and pencil to a nail located at the center-point, and mark the decking for a circular cut.

Rails and Top Cap for a Curved Railing

After you've installed and trimmed the decking, cut lengths of 2x8 and 2x12 for the rails and cap, and arrange them around the perimeter of the decking in the proper locations. Make them a bit longer than needed to start. On each piece, mark for the outside edge by running a pencil along the underside of the board, using the decking as a guide. Cut the boards to shape with a professional-quality saber saw, and then use a compass or scribe tool to mark the inside edge 3½ (rails) and 5½ inches (cap) in from the outside edge.

Curved Bench

Construct the 2x4 framing as shown in the drawing below, and then attach the fascia. It will curve in the middle, but it needn't follow the curve that the seat pieces will have.

Cut a number of seat pieces to the dimensions shown, and install them. They will measure a little longer than necessary. Make adjustments as you go, to ensure that you don't end up with a narrow or odd-shaped piece at the end. Make a final cut on both sides with a saber saw; then sand the edges smooth.

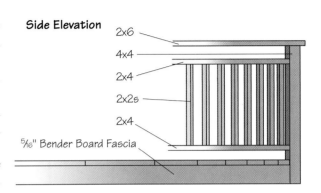

Side Elevation

2x6
4x4
2x4
2x2s
2x4
⁵⁄₁₆" Bender Board Fascia

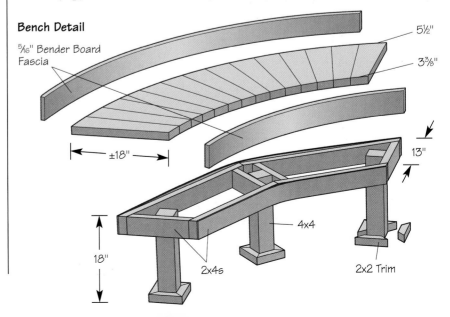

Bench Detail

⁵⁄₁₆" Bender Board Fascia

5½"
3⅜"
±18"
13"
18"
4x4
2x4s
2x2 Trim

Two Low Levels with Angles and an Overhead

*D*espite their flat yard and the low threshold into their home, these homeowners asked for a deck with at least two levels. To accommodate them, Parish came up with an unusual solution: a deck that rises above the house's floor level, rather than descending from it. Interesting angles, a bench/planter, and an elegant overhead structure make this a soothing place to relax.

Ground View

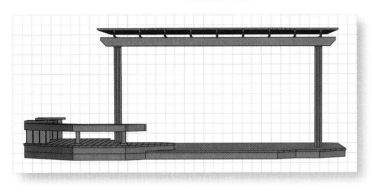

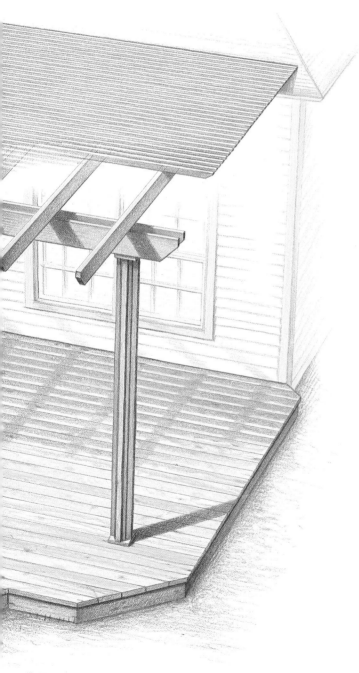

Design Considerations

The homeowners wanted to expand the area occupied by an existing rectangular concrete patio—and provide some shade at the same time. For structural reasons, Parish's design follows the shape of the patio, but has dressed up the deck with interesting features that effectively disguise its basic rectangular outline.

Although it has plenty of angles, the deck's perimeter makes use of theme and variation to avoid a jumbled or confused look For example, the forward section of the upper level, which angles away from the house at 45 degrees, parallels several other lines in the deck. By restating the theme in different ways, Parish avoids a ho-hum symmetrical effect but still ties the whole design together.

The main level offers plenty of room for a table with chairs and a grill, while the upper level provides a pleasant area for conversation, lounging, or just enjoying the foliage. The bench joins two planters that rise slightly above the seat level. With some fairly tall plants, this provides a naturally secluded place to sit and read. The benches form a semicircle of sorts, a shape that promotes conversation during a party.

The overhead structure is supported by "fluted" posts made of 4x4s and 2x2s. Though it requires only a bit of extra work and expense, this detail makes a big difference. An unadorned 4x4 post set in the middle of a deck would look drab and dreary; this variation adds grace and interest. The 2x2 roof pieces run north to south to provide maximum shade and are self-spaced (set $1^{1}/_{2}$ inches apart so that the gaps equal the width of the pieces). In a region that gets a lot of sun, the orientation and spacing of these top pieces requires serious planning. (See "Techniques to Use," page 162, for more information on this and on making "fluted" posts.)

Two Low Levels with Angles and an Overhead, Plan View

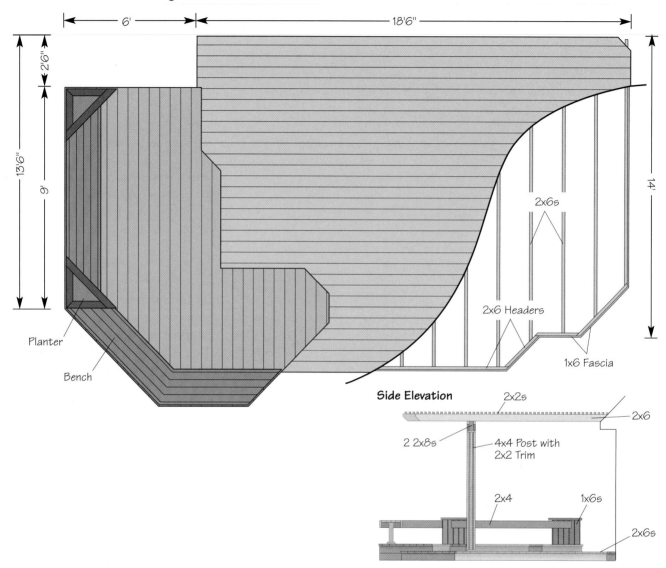

Planter

Bench

2x6s

2x6 Headers

1x6 Fascia

Side Elevation

2x2s

2x6

2 2x8s

4x4 Post with
2x2 Trim

2x4

1x6s

2x6s

Materials Used for This Deck and Overhead		
Framing	2x6 joists laid on a patio surface Shims	
Decking	2x6s	
Fascia	1x6s	
Overhead	4x4s and 2x2s for posts 2x8s for beams 2x6 rafters 2x2 top and bottom trim pieces	
Benches	4x4 posts 2x4 framing pieces 2x6 seat pieces	

	2x2 trim at bottom of posts	

Planters	Pressure-treated 2x4s, for bottom
	   plates and framing pieces
	Redwood 2x4s for top trim
	Tongue-and-groove redwood 1x6s,
	   clear all-heart, for sides
	Silicone caulk
	Pea gravel for bottom	

Hardware	Joist hangers for 2x6s Anchors to attach overhead to roof Fasteners for joist hangers 2½" and 3" deck screws	

Construction Techniques

If you don't have a patio surface on which to lay the joists, use standard framing techniques. On a deck this low, which doesn't allow room for a beam under the joists, you'll need to tie the joists to flush beams using joist hangers. For the overhead, figure out ahead of time exactly how you'll tie the rafters to the roof or eave.

Framing Over a Patio Surface. In Dallas, where frost heave is not a concern, Parish may simply lay the framing on top of an existing patio. If your area is subject to frost, the local building department will probably require that you dig footings that extend below the frost line. As an alternative, you may be able to build a *floating* deck that rises and falls a bit as the seasons change. *In that case, do not attach the framing to the house with a ledger board.* However, if you omit the ledger but still attach the overhead to the house, you run a risk of damaging the roof.

As long as you use 2x6 or larger joists, you needn't attach them to the concrete; just set them in place. If the threshold to the house sits so low that you're forced to use 2x4s or 2x2s, you may need to anchor them.

Orient the joists so that rainwater will flow easily beneath the deck. Most patios are sloped slightly for drainage, so this usually means setting the joists perpendicular to the house. As long as the slope is not severe, you may prefer simply to lay the joists on top and allow the deck slope as well. If you'd rather level the deck, build the framing and then use shims.

Overhead with Fluted Posts. Secure the posts to the deck framing using bolts. Add the 2x2 wraparound trim at the bottom (after decking) and near the top of the post; then position the members for the beams to rest on. Plumb the posts, temporarily brace them, and then add the beams. To add the fluting, attach a centered 2x2 to each face of all 4x4s.

Two rafters on each side measure 12 inches shorter than the middle rafters.

When installing the top pieces, allow the shorter, outermost pieces to run wild. Then, make chalk-line marks and trim them to length.

The Planters. Parish's planters sit directly on top of the decking, though he provides drainage by adding a generous layer of pea gravel at the bottom so that the decking can dry out. If your area stays wet for long periods, however, you may want to use another design.

Attach a frame of pressure-treated 2x4s to the deck, laid flat, and seal it with silicone caulk. Build a second frame as shown, using the same material. Clad the outside with clear, all-heart 1x6 tongue-and-groove redwood. For this application, any knots will cause problems. Like the sides of a hot tub, the redwood will expand and seal when it absorbs moisture. Cover the top with a cap of 2x4 redwood.

For drainage, pour in a layer of 6 or more inches of pea gravel. Add light soil that contains plenty of peat moss or other organic matter.

Overhead Detail

2x2s

2x6s

2 2x8s

2x2 Trim

"Fluted" Post

2x2 Trim

Post, Plan View

2x2

4x4

Planter Detail

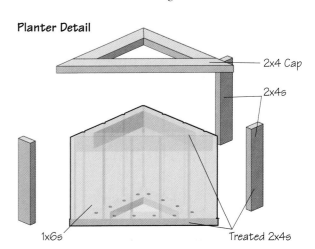

2x4 Cap

2x4s

1x6s

Treated 2x4s

Curves and More Curves

S pace was at a premium here, but the homeowners wanted two things: a set of steps descending from the house to the garage and a deck with some style and flair. Parish responded with a unique design using lots of curved lines.

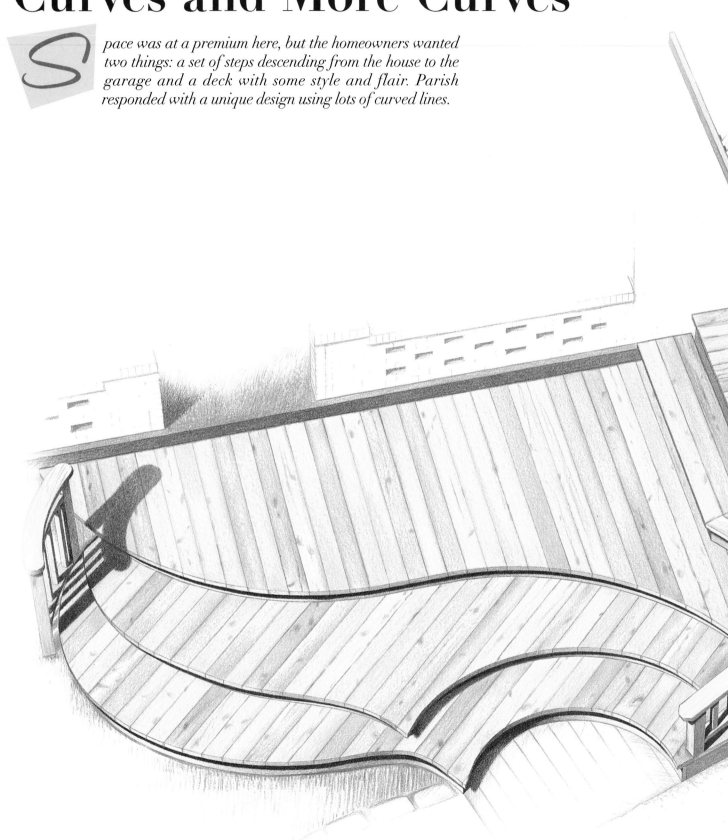

Ground View

Design Considerations

What do you do with a small yard? The usual solution: build a rectangular deck that uses every possible square inch. In other words, you sacrifice styling to gain usable space. Unfortunately, such a design often emphasizes the smallness of the yard—the deck looks as if it's been shoehorned into place.

But in this kind of situation, Parish often prefers to "waste" space with an unusual design. His logic? A deck with more pliant contours, one that doesn't seem frantic about grabbing all the space it possibly can, will give the yard a more relaxed atmosphere.

With this design, however, Parish went far beyond unusual. At a glance, this deck appears to waste extravagant amounts of space. Yet the seemingly haphazard shapes disguise a deck that does a number of practical jobs. When family members take the most direct path from the house's back door to the garage (something they do often), they descend on steps that measure a uniform 16 inches long. Such uniformity makes stepping down feel more natural and takes safety into account as well: When carrying groceries, you often can't see the steps, and it helps to know that they all have the same depth.

While the deck's main level does not provide room for a standard round table with four chairs, it easily accommodates several diners sitting around three sides of a rectangular table. These homeowners don't often barbecue or throw large parties, so it suits their needs fine. They make use of the multiple levels to arrange flowerpots and prefer having the interesting lines instead of all that "usable" space that they wouldn't use.

Curves and More Curves, Plan View

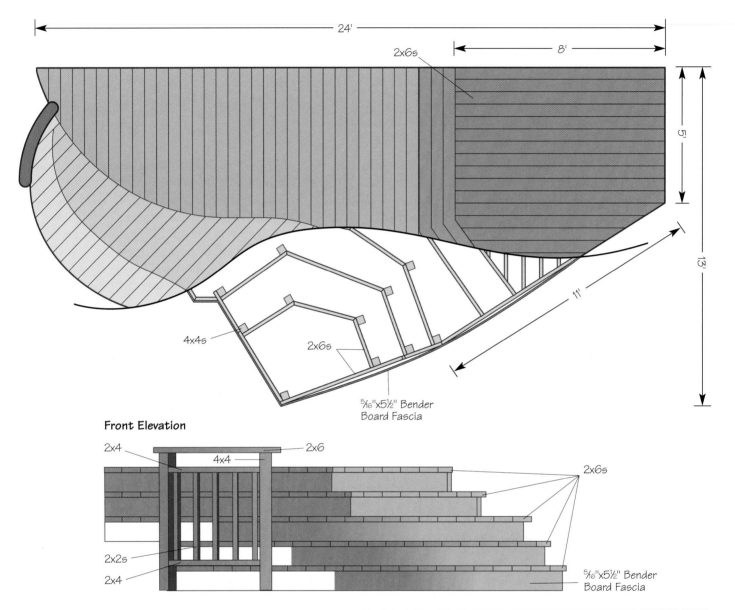

Front Elevation

Materials Used for This Deck

Framing	4x4 posts 2x6 joists 2x2 spacers			2x2 balusters 2x6 railing cap (cut from 2x12s)
			Trivet	1x2s
Decking	2x6s			
			Hardware	Joist hangers for 2x6s Fasteners for joist hangers 3" deck screws 2½" deck screws
Fascia	5⁄16"x5½" bender board (cut from 2x6s)			
Railing	4x4 posts 2x4 rails (cut from 2x8s)		Masonry	Concrete for footings

Construction Techniques

It's virtually impossible to draw and then build a deck with this many curves to exact specifications. But you can come close. In this case, the only part of the project that requires exacting construction is the pathway down to the garage, which calls for steps that are all uniform in height and depth.

Laying Out and Framing Curved Deck Lines

Use a thick rope or garden hose—something that will bend smoothly—to lay out the curves. You may prefer to stiffen the hose by capping its end and turning on the water. This improves the curve and makes the hose easier to use. Lay out the curved lines on the ground, using a tape measure to verify that the lines are properly distanced from one another and a stake-and-string compass to check the curves for uniformity.

After you've properly located the hose, pour flour or sand along its length. When you pick it up, it will leave a clearly defined line.

To determine the best layout for perimeter framing, arrange lengths of 2x4 on the ground. No piece should cross the outline of the deck, but neither should any piece fall more than 3 inches short of it. Use this method to locate your postholes.

Dig the postholes, going below the frost line if necessary, and set the posts in them, leaving them longer than they need to be. Plumb the posts and install temporary supports. (See the illustration for a layout example.)

Cut and install the joist pieces. If you're using 2x6 joists and want the steps to measure 7 inches high, use 2x2s to space them as shown. (For 8³/₄-inch risers, use 2x8 joists.)

Once you've framed the perimeters, complete the framing by installing joists that run perpendicular to the way the decking will run. Pour the concrete for the footings, and allow it to set fully. Add the bender-board fascia, taking care to get smooth curves. Install the decking, allowing it to overhang by 1½ inches or so. Use a professional-quality saber saw to cut the final curves.

Trivet for Flowerpots

Set a flowerpot on even the most rot-resistant decking, and within a year it will produce stains that are difficult to remove. Parish recommends using a simple trivet like the one shown. He makes the little stands entirely out of 1x2s, rounding off the top edges of the top pieces with a router and roundover bit.

Framing for Curves

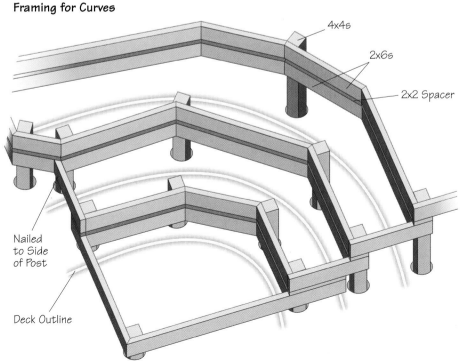

4x4s

2x6s

2x2 Spacer

Nailed
to Side
of Post

Deck Outline

Trivet Detail

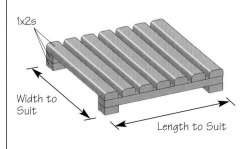

1x2s

Width to
Suit

Length to Suit

Pagoda Platform

he homeowners wanted a decorative element in their yard, something with an Asian touch. A small deck with three steps merely serves as a platform for the main attraction: an ornate overhead structure that would look right at home in a Japanese rock garden.

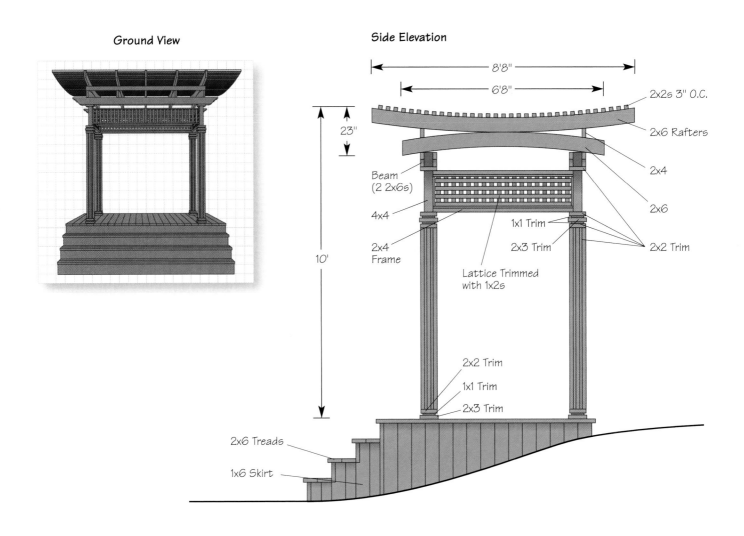

Ground View

Side Elevation

8'8"

6'8"

23"

10'

2x2s 3" O.C.

2x6 Rafters

2x4

2x6

2x2 Trim

Beam
(2 2x6s)

4x4

2x4
Frame

1x1 Trim

2x3 Trim

Lattice Trimmed
with 1x2s

2x2 Trim

1x1 Trim

2x3 Trim

2x6 Treads

1x6 Skirt

Design Considerations

This freestanding deck offers enough room for a small table with chairs or for several lounge chairs. More important, it provides eye-catching ornamentation for the yard, a welcome alternative to the conventional prefabricated decorative structure. It conveys an Asian sense of grace and serenity rather than the usual Victorian or gingerbread-house charm of a gazebo.

Wide steps lead up to the simple, rectangular deck. Include the steps only if the site is sloped, as it was at the site for which this design was conceived. If you build this deck to rise 28 inches or so above a flat yard, it will look silly. Any steps that you use should nearly follow the contour of the landscape.

The elaborate overhead structure draws the eye upward. Fluted posts reach up to a lattice enclosure that supports beams with wing-like ends. Atop these beams sit double rafters, one curving downward and the other upward, that appear to balance precariously. Horizontal supports made from 2x4s provide additional support for the curved rafters. Top pieces of 2x2 provide shade and give a partial sense of enclosure.

This design depends on small touches and careful craftsmanship for its overall effect. At the point where the upper and lower curved rafters meet, Parish added a detail (made of 2x2s and 1x1s) that resembles a rope, which Japanese joiners traditionally used to tie frame members together. For the beam ends, he used a traditional profile that is ornate but not flashy, and the abundance of small joints enhances the Asian feel of the structure.

Pagoda Platform and Pergola, Plan View

Pergola Plan View

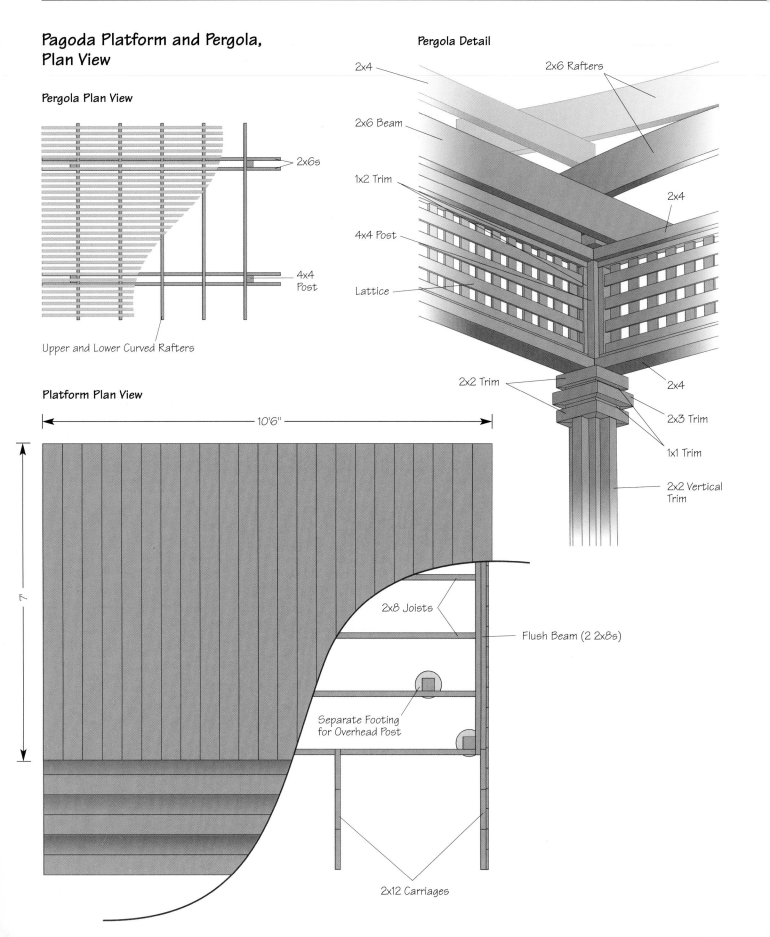

2x6s

4x4 Post

Upper and Lower Curved Rafters

Pergola Detail

2x4

2x6 Rafters

2x6 Beam

1x2 Trim

4x4 Post

Lattice

2x4

2x4

2x2 Trim

2x3 Trim

1x1 Trim

2x2 Vertical Trim

Platform Plan View

10'6"

7'

2x8 Joists

Flush Beam (2 2x8s)

Separate Footing for Overhead Post

2x12 Carriages

Construction Techniques

Use standard footings and posts for the deck. Tie the joists to flush beams made of doubled 2x8s. Build the steps to standard dimensions, using a rise and run of about 7 and 11 inches, respectively. Use carriages every 32 inches or so.

Overhead with Double-Curved Rafters. Unless you have the patience to do careful—even fussy—carpentry, you should probably turn this job over to a professional. And don't hire anyone who can't show evidence of advanced joinery skills. Select only the best lumber, at least B-grade heart redwood that is dry

and free of warps and splits. Sloppy work or blemished lumber will stick out like a sore thumb on this structure.

Use a router and roundover bit to give all trim pieces a uniformly rounded edge.

Sink the posts into deep holes, plumb them carefully, and then pour the concrete, allowing it to set completely before proceeding. Cut the posts to height, and trim them with the 2x3s, 2x2s, and 1x1s as shown. (Make the latter by ripping any ³/₄-inch-thick stock to ³/₄ inch wide.) Build a 2x4

frame for the lattice sections, and sandwich the lattice using 1x2 trim pieces.

Before you cut the wing-like ends on the 2x6 beams, experiment on a scrap piece of lumber. Use a compass to draw the intersecting arcs; then cut them using a professional-quality saber saw. Once you've found the design you like, use it as a template for all of the beam cuts. Now, attach the lattice sections, the upper 2x2 trim, and the beams to the posts.

To cut the curved rafters, you'll again want to experiment to find a profile that suits your tastes. Start by setting

Curved Rafter Detail

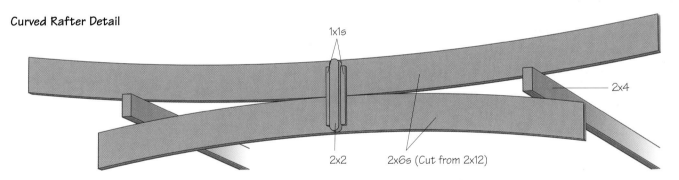

1x1s

2x4

2x2   2x6s (Cut from 2x12)

Materials Used for This Deck and Pergola

Framing	Double 2x8 beam 4x4 posts 2x8 joists		1x1 trim pieces Prefabricated lattice panels 1x2 trim for lattice 2x6s for beams (two for each beam) 2x12s for upper and lower curved rafters 2x4 horizontal supports 2x2s and 1x1s for "rope" trim 2x2 top pieces
Decking	2x6s		
Skirting	1x6s		
Steps	2x12 stringers 2x6 treads (2 for each step) 1x8 risers		
		Hardware	Joist hangers for 2x8s Fasteners for joist hangers 2½" deck screws 3" deck screws
Overhead	4x4s and 2x2s for posts 2x3 trim pieces 2x2 trim pieces		

a 2x12 on the ground and anchoring it so that it won't move. Fix a point about 10 feet from the board, and then tack a nail there to serve as the centerpoint of the arc. Tie a string and pencil to the nail, and mark a curved line along the bottom of the rafter. If this arc looks good, measure back from the line 5½ inches and mark a parallel line for the top of the rafter.

Cut the profile to shape, and then rout the edges smooth using a roundover bit. (Or sand them using a belt sander.) Use the first rafter as a template for the others.

Cut the elements of the "rope" trim out of 2x2s and 1x1s. Next, arrange two of the curved rafters on the ground, and attach a rope trim to both

sides. This will tie them together securely enough that, with a helper and two good ladders, you can raise the paired rafters into position on top of the beams. (If possible, do this on a windless day.) Measure carefully to make sure they're centered, and then attach the lower rafters to the beams with angle-driven screws. Add the 2x4 horizontal supports and the top 2x2s.

Bridge and Lamp

These two amiable touches will harmonize with a variety of deck styles. Even if you don't have a stream on your property, the bridge adds a dramatic decorative effect, and the lamppost has ornamental appeal as well as functional value.

In combination with the "Pagoda Platform" (page 180), the bridge and lamp clearly evoke their Far Eastern origins. But in other settings the structures can assume different identities. The bridge can take on rustic overtones that recall rural America, while the lamppost's shape resembles that of classic carriage-house designs.

Construction Techniques

Because these projects are on the small side, you may be able to use scrap lumber for most of the parts.

Bridge. Round over all the pieces, including the top edges of the treads,

Arched Bridge

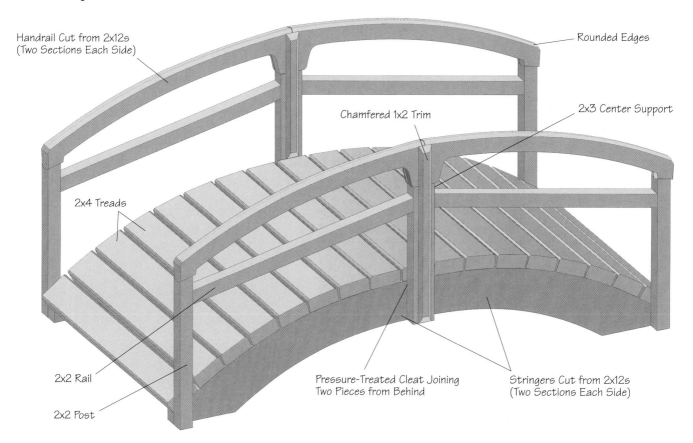

Handrail Cut from 2x12s
(Two Sections Each Side)

Rounded Edges

Chamfered 1x2 Trim

2x3 Center Support

2x4 Treads

2x2 Rail

2x2 Post

Pressure-Treated Cleat Joining
Two Pieces from Behind

Stringers Cut from 2x12s
(Two Sections Each Side)

using a belt sander or a router equipped with a roundover bit. The more you round the railing edges, the more they will resemble logs. To enhance this rustic look, round over the lumber somewhat unevenly.

Determine the length and curve you want, using large pieces of cardboard or scraps of wood cobbled together. With a pencil-and-string compass, mark for the cuts on one of the stringer pieces. After you cut it, use this stringer as a template for the other three and as a guide for cutting the handrails.

Tie the stringers together using cleats and screws from the back. Drill pilot holes to make sure you don't split the wood. Cut and attach the treads; then assemble the railing.

Lamp. Set the 4x4 post in at least 12 inches of concrete so that it will withstand a bump or two. Run the low-voltage cable to the post in a shallow trench, or simply cover it with mulch, gravel, or topsoil. To make a pathway for the cable into the light housing, cut a groove in the inside face of one of the vertical 2x2s and one of the 2x2 trim pieces. Drill a hole in the 2x8 bottom flat piece for the cable, and attach the light.

Cut the 2x2 uprights to the desired height. Next, crosscut the 1x6 and 1x2 housing pieces to length, and assemble them. Glue the lenses in place; then attach the housing to the 2x8 by screwing from underneath. Attach the 2x2 trim, and then the assembled housing. Caulk all joints with a small bead of clear silicone caulk, and add the two top pieces. Use only one or two screws on the 1x10 top piece, so you'll be able to remove it to change lightbulbs.

Outdoor Lamppost

Lamppost Detail

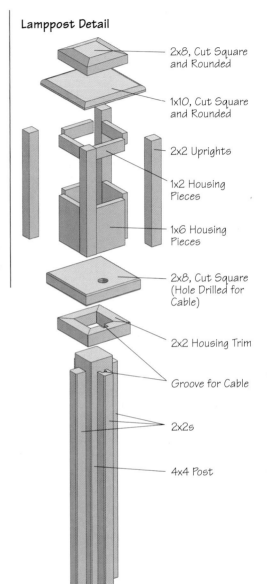

2x8, Cut Square and Rounded

1x10, Cut Square and Rounded

2x2 Uprights

1x2 Housing Pieces

1x6 Housing Pieces

2x8, Cut Square (Hole Drilled for Cable)

2x2 Housing Trim

Groove for Cable

2x2s

4x4 Post

Materials Used for Bridge and Lamppost

Bridge	2x12s for stringers Pressure-treated plywood for stringer cleats 2x4 treads 2x12s or 2x10s for handrails 2x2 rails and posts 2x3 center supports 1x2 trim		1x2 housing pieces 2x2s for light housing 1x6 housing pieces Translucent plastic for light-housing lenses (from a 2'x2' piece intended for use as a hung-ceiling panel) 2x8s for bottom flat piece and top cap 1x10 for next-to-the-top flat piece
Light	Low-voltage light fixture, with housing removed 4x4 post 2x2 post and housing trim	Hardware	3" deck screws 2" deck screws
		Masonry	Concrete

Directory of Deck Railings & More

Railings

Page 49

Page 89

Pages 52–53

Page 117

Page 59

Page 129

Page 67

Pages 144–45

Pages 72–73

Pages 148–49

Planters

Pages 62–63

Page 85

Page 105

Page 175

Pages 152–53

Pergolas

Page 53

Page 63

Pages 133–35

Pages 182–84

Page 157

Benches

Page 53

Pages 72–73

Page 85

Page 97

Page 111

Page 171

Actual dimensions The exact measurements of a piece of lumber after it has been cut, surfaced, and dried. For example, a 2×4's actual dimensions are 1½×3½ inches.

Balusters The numerous vertical pieces, often made of 2×2s or 1×4s, that fill in spaces between rails and provide a fence-like structure.

Band joist Any joist that defines the perimeter of a deck, including the header joist and end, or outside, joists. Also called rim joist.

Beam A large framing member, usually four-by material or doubled-up two-bys, which is attached horizontally to the posts and used to support joists.

Blocking Usually solid pieces of lumber, the same dimensions as the joists, which are cut to fit snugly between the joists to prevent excessive warping. Also called bridging or bracing.

Building codes Municipal rules regulating safe building practices and procedures. Generally, the codes encompass structural, electrical, plumbing, and mechanical remodeling and new construction. Confirmation of conformity to local codes by inspection may be required.

Building permit A license that authorizes permission to do work on your home. Minor repairs and remodeling work usually do not call for a permit, but if the job consists of extending the water supply and drain, waste, vent system; adding an electrical circuit; or making structural changes to a building, a building permit may be necessary.

Cantilever Construction that extends beyond its vertical support.

Curing The slow chemical action that hardens concrete.

Decking Boards nailed to joists to form the deck surface.

Elevation Architectural drawing of a structure seen from the side, rear, or front view.

Fascia board Facing that covers the exposed ends and sides of decking to provide a finished appearance.

Footing The concrete base that supports posts or steps.

Frost line The maximum depth to which soil freezes. The local building department can provide information on the frost line depth in your area.

Grade The ground level. On-grade means at or on the natural ground level.

Header joist Band joist attached and running at a right angle to common joists, enabling them to maintain correct spacing and stiffening their ends.

Joist Structural member, usually two-by lumber, commonly placed perpendicularly across beams to support deck boards.

Joist hanger Metal connector used to join a joist and beam so that the tops are in the same plane.

Knot The high-density root of a limb that is very dense but is not connected to the surrounding wood.

Lag screw Large wood screw (usually ¼ inch or more in diameter) with a bolt-like hex head usually used to attached ledgers to house framing. Often incorrectly called lag bolt.

Lattice A cross-pattern structure that is made of wood, metal, or plastic.

Ledger Horizontal board attached to the side of a house or wall to support a deck or an overhead cover.

Nominal dimensions The identifying dimensions of a piece of lumber (e.g. 2×4) which are larger than the actual dimensions (1½×3½).

Penny (abbreviated "d") Unit of measurement for nail length; e.g., a 10d nail is 3 inches long.

Permanent structure Any structure that is anchored to the ground or a house.

Plan drawing A drawing which gives an overhead view of the deck showing where all footings and lumber pieces go.

Plumb Vertically straight, in relation to a horizontally level surface.

Plunge cut A cut that can't begin from the outside of the board and must be made from the middle.

Post A vertical member, usually 4×4 or 6×6, that supports either the deck or railing.

Post anchor A metal fastener designed to keep the post from wandering and also to inhibit rot by holding the post a bit above the concrete.

Posthole digger A clamshell-type tool used to dig holes for posts.

Power auger A tool that is powered by a gasoline engine and used for drilling into the ground. Often used in larger projects to dig postholes.

Pressure-treated lumber Wood that has had preservatives forced into it under pressure to make it repel rot and insects.

On center A point of reference for measuring. For example, "16 inches on center" means 16 inches from the center of one framing member to the center of the next.

Rabbet A ledge cut along one edge of a workpiece.

Rail A horizontal member that is placed between posts and used for support or as a barrier.

Railing Assembly made from balusters attached to rails and installed between posts as a safety barrier at the edge of a deck.

Railing cap A horizontal piece of lumber laid flat on top of the post and top rail, covering the end grain of the post and providing a flat surface wide enough to set objects on.

Recommended span The distance a piece of lumber can safely traverse without being supported underneath.

Redwood A straight-grain, weather-resistant wood used for outdoor building.

Rim joist *See* Band joist.

Rip cut A cut made with the grain on a piece of wood.

Riser Vertical boards placed between stringers on stairs to support stair treads. They are optional on exterior stairs.

Site plan A drawing which maps out your house and yard. Also called a base plan.

Skewing Driving two nails at opposing angles. This technique creates a sounder connection by "hooking" the boards together as well as by reducing the possibility of splitting.

Skirt Solid band of horizontal wood members (fascia) installed around the deck perimeter to conceal exposed ends of joists and deck boards.

Stringer On stairs, the diagonal boards that support the treads and risers; also called a stair horse.

Tack-nail To nail one structural member to another temporarily with a minimal amount of nails.

Toenail Joining two boards together by nailing at an angle through the end, or toe, on one board and into the face of another.

Tread On stairs, the horizontal boards supported by the stringers.

Safety Considerations

Though all the designs and methods in this book have been reviewed for safety, it is not possible to overstate the importance of using the safest construction methods possible. What follows are reminders—some do's and don'ts of basic carpentry. They are not substitutes for your own common sense.

- *Always* use caution, care, and good judgment when following the procedures described in this book.

- *Always* be sure that the electrical setup is safe; be sure that no circuit is overloaded, and that all power tools and electrical outlets are properly grounded. Do not use power tools in wet locations.

- *Always* read container labels on paints, solvents, and other products; provide ventilation, and observe all other warnings.

- *Always* read the tool manufacturer's instructions for using a tool, especially the warnings.

- *Always* remove the key from any drill chuck (portable or press) before starting the drill.

- *Always* know the limitations of your tools. Do not try to force them to do what they were not designed to do.

- *Always* make sure that any adjustment is locked before proceeding.

- *Always* wear the appropriate rubber or work gloves when handling chemicals, doing heavy construction, or sanding.

- *Always* wear a disposable face mask when working around odors, dust, or mist. Use a special filtering respirator when working with toxic substances.

- *Always* wear eye protection, especially when using power tools or striking metal on metal or concrete.

- *Always* keep your hands away from the business ends of blades, cutters, and bits.

- *Always* check your local building codes when planning new construction. The codes are intended to protect public safety.

- *Never* work with power tools when you are tired or under the influence of alcohol or drugs.

- *Never* cut very small pieces of wood or pipe. Whenever possible, cut small pieces off larger pieces.

- *Never* change a blade or a bit unless the power cord is unplugged.

- *Never* work while wearing loose clothing, hanging hair, open cuffs, or jewelry.

- *Never* use a power tool on a workpiece that is not firmly supported or clamped.

- *Never* support a workpiece from underneath with your leg or other part of your body when sawing.

- *Never* carry sharp or pointed tools, such as utility knives, awls, or chisels, in your pocket. If you want to carry tools, use a special-purpose tool belt with leather pockets and holders.

Metric Equivalents

All measurements in this book are given in U.S. Customary units. If you wish to find metric equivalents, use the following tables and conversion factors.

Inches to Millimeters and Centimeters

1 in = 25.4 mm = 2.54 cm

in	mm	cm
1/16	1.5875	0.1588
1/8	3.1750	0.3175
1/4	6.3500	0.6350
3/8	9.5250	0.9525
1/2	12.7000	1.2700
5/8	15.8750	1.5875
3/4	19.0500	1.9050
7/8	22.2250	2.2225
1	25.4000	2.5400

Inches to Centimeters and Meters

1 in = 2.54 cm = 0.0254 m

in	cm	m
1	2.54	0.0254
2	5.08	0.0508
3	7.62	0.0762
4	10.16	0.1016
5	12.70	0.1270
6	15.24	0.1524
7	17.78	0.1778
8	20.32	0.2032
9	22.86	0.2286
10	25.40	0.2540
11	27.94	0.2794
12	30.48	0.3048

Feet to Meters

1 ft = 0.3048 m

ft	m
1	0.3048
5	1.5240
10	3.0480
25	7.6200
50	15.2400
100	30.4800

Square Feet to Square Meters

1 ft² = 0.092 903 04 m²

Acres to Square Meters

1 acre = 4046.85642 m²

Cubic Yards to Cubic Meters

1 yd³ = 0.764 555 m³

Ounces and Pounds (Avoirdupois) to Grams

1 oz = 28.349 523 g

1 lb = 453.5924 g

Pounds to Kilograms

1 lb = 0.453 592 37 k

Ounces and Quarts to Liters

1 oz = 0.029 573 53 l

1 qt = 0.9463 l

Gallons to Liters

1 gal = 3.785 411 784 l

Fahrenheit to Celsius (Centigrade)

$°C = °F - 32 \times 5/9$

°F	°C
-30	-34.45
-20	-28.89
-10	-23.34
-5	-20.56
0	-17.78
10	-12.22
20	-6.67
30	-1.11
32 (freezing)	0.00
40	4.44
50	10.00
60	15.56
70	21.11
80	26.67
90	32.22
100	37.78
212 (boiling)	100

Nail Sizes (penny, inch)

2d–1"	6d–2"	10d–3"	30d–4½"
3d–1¼"	7d–2¼"	12d–3¼"	40d–5"
4d–1½"	8d–2½"	16d–3½"	50d–5½"
5d–1¾"	9d–2¾"	20d–4"	60d–6"

Have a home improvement, decorating, or gardening project? Look for these and other fine Creative Homeowner books wherever books are sold.

Step-by-step deck building for the novice. Over 500 photos and illustrations. 192 pp.; 8½"×10⅞"
BOOK#: 277162

Covers the newest deck design, built-ins, and add-ons. Over 250 color photos. 128 pp.; 8½"×10⅞"
BOOK#: 277155

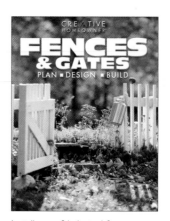

Install a prefabricated fence, or build your own. Over 350 color photos. 144 pp.; 8½"×10⅞"
BOOK #: 277985

Design ideas, planning advice, and step-by-step projects. 460 color photos, illustrations. 160 pp.; 8½"×10⅞"
BOOK#: 274804

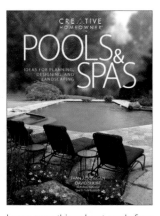

Learn everything about pools, from planning to installation. 300 color photos. 224 pp.; 8½"×10⅞"
BOOK#: 277853

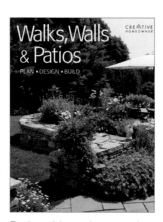

Design advice and construction techniques. 500+ color photos, illustrations. 240 pp. 8½"×10⅞"
BOOK#: 277997

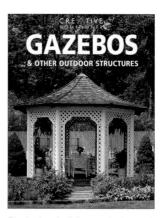

Designing, building techniques for yard structures. 450+ color photos, illustrations. 160 pp.; 8½"×10⅞"
BOOK#: 277138

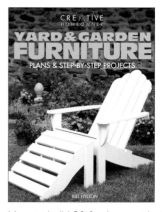

How to build 20 furniture projects. 470+ color photos, illustrations. 208 pp.; 8½"×10⅞"
BOOK#: 277462

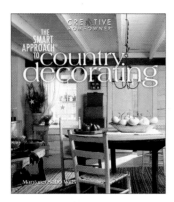

Fill your home with the spirit of country. More than 200 photos. 176 pp.; 9"×10"
BOOK #: 279685

How to work with space, color, pattern, texture. Over 400 photos. 288 pp.; 9"×10"
BOOK #: 279672

An impressive guide to garden design and plant selection. More than 600 color photos. 320 pp.; 9"×10"
BOOK #: 274615

Lavishly illustrated with portraits of over 100 flowering plants; more than 500 photos. 208 pp.; 9"×10"
BOOK #: 274032

For more information, and to order direct, call 800-631-7795; in New Jersey 201-934-7100.
www.creativehomeowner.com